WORSHIP QUEST

WORSHIP QUEST

An Exploration of Worship Leadership

STEVEN D. BROOKS

foreword by
JIM ALTIZER

WIPF & STOCK · Eugene, Oregon

WORSHIP QUEST
An Exploration of Worship Leadership

Wipf and Stock
An Imprint of Wipf and Stock Publishers
199 W. 8th Ave., Suite 3
Eugene, OR 97401

www.wipfandstock.com

ISBN 13: 978-1-62564-920-1

Manufactured in the U.S.A.   02/13/2015

You have made us for yourself, oh God;
And our hearts are restless until they rest in you.

AUGUSTINE OF HIPPO

Be sure to check out Worship Quest Ministries.

Worship resources designed to encourage and enhance worship renewal within the church.

www.worshipquestministries.com

Contents

Appendices

Foreword

WARNING! THIS BOOK WILL challenge and change you. I have watched Dr. Steven Brooks develop through graduate school into a full-fledged Professor of Worship Leadership, and he knows, intimately, that of which he writes. If you want worship philosophy, you will find it here. If you want some practical tools, you will find them here as well. Dr. Brooks cracks open his diary and gives us a peek at his journey toward loving and leading the body of Christ in worship, and it is fascinating. His insights into the various types of worship gatherings will answer a lot of questions about why things are the way they are in the local Church. Steven is a godly man, a good scholar and a practical theologian who is immersed in that of which he speaks and writes. Enjoy and learn!

—Dr. Jim Altizer
Azusa Pacific University

Preface

It is in the process of being worshipped that
God communicates his presence to men.

C.S. LEWIS

I FIND THAT SOME of my best teaching, and hopefully for my students, some of their best learning, occurs in the midst of dialogue. On one particular evening, my class was engaged in a lively discussion on worship leadership. We talked about the importance of knowing and understanding the various roles in which leaders of worship are called to serve. We discussed the responsibilities of the worship leadership roles and the confusion and frustration that accompany not serving in the correct role. We also discussed how the different roles function within various worship gatherings. It was a dynamic discussion that concluded with one of my students declaring, "This is great! You should write a book about all this." The rest of the class unanimously agreed. The book you are holding in your hands is a result of that class discussion.

We are all on a quest when it comes to worship. There are so many questions and oftentimes, too many opinions, when it comes to the topic of worship. As you picked up this book, I'm sure you came with your own preconceived ideas and opinions formed by tradition and experience. You may even possess a certain level of education on the topic obtained from academic institutions, conferences, churches, etc. Regardless, I trust that the fact that you even picked up this book in the first place indicates your awareness that there is always more God wants to teach us about how to respond to Him through worship. My hope is that after reading this book you will walk away with a greater understanding of worship leadership while accepting that there is always much more to discover. The journey of learning to worship well is a lifelong process. Some of the questions we have regarding worship will never find their answers this side of heaven.

So, with the surplus of questions and opinions that have developed over time, how can we figure out what it means to worship God in "spirit and truth" (John 4:24); in ways that honor, glorify and bless his name? There are some who say that if you just read the Bible you will know how to worship God, but is it really that simple? What exactly does the Bible teach us about worship? Perhaps a better way to ask that would be what does the Bible show us about worship? A look throughout the pages of Scripture shows us a variety of worship practices.

In the Old Testament, Abraham built altars to offer sacrifices to Yahweh. Moses introduced new elements of worship including songs, festivals, the reading of God's covenant, sprinkling with the "blood of the covenant", receiving offerings, and the building of the tabernacle. King David danced with all his might at the return of the Ark of the Covenant. His whole-hearted life of worship led to the writing of the Psalms, which have lasted for centuries and still encourage us in our worship today. Solomon knelt before the entire assembly as he cried out to the Lord. Jehoshaphat led the nation of Israel in prayer before sending the singers (the worship leaders) to the front line of battle. These are just a few examples found in the Old Testament.

If that weren't enough, worship in the New Testament provides us with even more diversity of worship practice. The early church[1] is exhorted to sing songs, pray, read Scripture, preach and teach the Word, collect offerings, baptize and observe the Lord's Supper. The church in Acts practiced communal living. The apostle Paul speaks to the Corinthians about their charismatic ways encouraging them to speak in tongues, interpret tongues, sing in the Spirit, and perform miracles.

1. I use the word "church" throughout this book as a means for describing the gathered body of Christ, the *ecclesia*. As Christians, we know the church is the people and not a building. In order to maintain consistency and try to avoid confusion, I have decided to use the word most commonly associated with the gathered body of Christ, that is, "church." When I capitalize the first letter, as in "Church," I mean the global, universal Church made up of those around the world whom gather to worship the Lord (names of churches would be an exception). When I intend to speak of the building in which we gather for worship, I will say "church building" or "facilities."

Anyone who looks to the Bible to find a specific pattern of worship will be sorely disappointed. In fact, we find just the opposite. Worship throughout the Bible varies according to culture, location and time period. Regardless of the diversity of worship practices, one thing is sure: God makes it clear that He is searching the earth, looking for worshipers:

> But the hour is coming, and is now here, when the true worshipers will worship the Father in spirit and truth, for the Father is seeking such people to worship him. (John 4:23)

The question then that must be asked is, what is a worshiper? Simply put, a worshiper of God is someone who has experienced his saving grace and responds accordingly. Worship is response. Think about it . . . God sent His only Son to be the once for all sacrifice for you and me. When we actually consider that truth, when we realize all God has done for us, and see him for Who he is, we can't help but worship.

Countless worship services are being planned and implemented around the world every day. Across the globe saints are gathering with the primary purpose of offering praise and worship to Almighty God. The songs of the redeemed and the prayers of the saints are being lifted to the Lord in an attempt to glorify the King of kings and Lord of lords. It is a great honor and privilege to gather together in worship. But how are these corporate gatherings planned and implemented? Moreover, are the right people in the right positions in order to accurately perform the duties of planning and leading worship services?

I have the privilege of planning and leading congregational worship as well as teaching worship ministry in university and seminary settings. My greatest passion is to train, mentor and equip ministry leaders. It is my desire to see the Church strengthened through worship renewal by gaining a greater understanding of biblical worship and returning Christ to his rightful place at the center of our worship.

When I began serving in ministry I had a limited understanding of worship. I grew up attending a small church and my understanding of worship during those years was that worship was music. We had worship and then the sermon. Music at this particular church, like many small churches during that era, consisted of an untrained volunteer music director leading the congregation in hymns from the hymnal. The singing was accompanied by organ and piano. The twenty-person choir would occasionally perform a song during the collection of the offering and, twice a year, would perform a Christmas and an Easter cantata (there's a word we don't hear anymore) to a pre-recorded accompaniment track.[2]

When I was in high school I was asked to lead worship for our youth group. This eventually led to my team introducing contemporary worship music to the church, as we would occasionally be asked to lead songs in "big church." I vividly remember a Sunday evening when some friends and I introduced a relatively new praise song called "Awesome God."[3]

Since those early days of volunteer music and worship ministry, my desire to learn how to best respond to God through worship has steadily grown. It has led me to pursue leading worship as a field of study and as a career. I am honored to have the opportunity to lead worship in church and teach worship ministry to the future generation of worship and ministry leaders.

I believe discussions on worship are some of the most important conversations we can have as followers of Christ for "surely that which occupies the total time and energies of heaven must be a fitting pattern for earth."[4] If we are going to worship for the rest of our lives (physical and eternal), shouldn't we do our best to understand how to worship properly?

I write this book with a primary target in mind, but hope it will have an impact beyond the scope of that target. My intent is for this book to positively influence those in worship leadership, whether you are presently leading worship or want to learn more about the privilege of doing so, as well as church leaders who desire to understand the roles of worship leadership in ministry. I believe by understanding the different worship gatherings and the various roles of worship leadership, one has a better chance of successfully fulfilling God's call of leading in worship. Additionally, my desire is that this book will serve as a foundation for those who simply want to know more about worship, regardless of whether or not you are currently serving in the worship ministry of a church.

The distinction of this book is that it provides a practical perspective on four roles of worship leadership and how they are to be fulfilled within various worship types and worship gatherings. There is much confusion among churches and those called to worship leadership when it comes to the topics discussed in this book. Many serving in church worship

2. When I say "track," what I mean is a cassette tape. If you don't know what a cassette tape is, you can Google it.

3. "Awesome God" Rich Mullins ©1986 BMG Songs, Inc.

4. Billheimer, *Destined For The Throne*, 116.

ministries are frustrated because they do not understand the different worship leadership roles and are attempting to fulfill a role that they are not necessarily called by God to fulfill. In other words, they are not working within their giftedness. Moreover, churches have placed improper expectations upon those in worship leadership because the church does not understand the difference between the worship leadership roles. Each role serves a different purpose in the body of Christ and we must understand the various roles and gatherings of worship if we are to successfully fulfill the role in which we have been called. My hope is that this book will help church leadership and those called to serve in worship leadership avoid confusion, disappointment and possible conflict because of the misunderstanding of roles and callings.

Before discussing the four roles of worship leadership, we will begin by looking at the foundations of worship (Part One). Answering these foundational questions will help us establish the groundwork for why various roles of worship leadership are even necessary in the first place. We will then take a look at the three types of worship that every Christian should practice (Part Two), as well as the four different worship gatherings in which we have the opportunity to participate (Part Three). We will conclude by considering the four roles of worship leadership (Part Four). Each chapter of these worship leadership roles will offer a practical perspective on how the four roles are to be fulfilled within varying worship types and worship gatherings.

On the first day of class I jokingly tell my students, "I will spend a whole semester teaching you about worship and when we get to heaven we'll probably find out that I was completely wrong. But for now, since I am the professor, just assume I'm right." My intention with this book is not to say, "I'm right. You're wrong," but instead, "let's journey together as we explore who God is, how he desires to be worshiped, and how we can best fulfill our roles of leading others in worship." My desire is that those called to lead in worship will begin to understand how God is calling them and those seeking worship leaders for their churches or organizations will learn better ways to discern whom they should place in worship leadership.

PART ONE
Foundations of Worship

All the nations you have made will come and worship before you, O Lord; they will bring glory to your name. For you are great and do marvelous deeds; you alone are God.

PSALM 86:9–10

BEFORE BEGINNING ANY DISCUSSION on the topic of worship, it is vital to ask some important questions regarding worship in general. What is worship? Whom should we worship? Where should we worship? Why should we worship? Who is welcome to worship? How should we worship? Understanding the answers to these questions establishes a foundation for participating in further pertinent worship discussions.

1

What Is Worship?

I can safely say, on the authority of all that is revealed in the Word of God, that any man or woman on this earth who is bored and turned off by worship is not ready for heaven.

A. W. TOZER

IF WORSHIPERS ARE TO accomplish the action of worship, shouldn't they first know what the word means? Over the centuries, theologians, biblical scholars and everyday worshipers have attempted to come up with a definition of worship. As a result, countless definitions have surfaced over time.[1] Many of these definitions have been based on biblical study, theological understanding, self–realization, or traditions that have been passed down from one generation to the next.

The reason for the variety of definitions for worship is because the Bible never provides us with a formal definition. There are numerous descriptions of worship throughout the pages of Scripture, but never a definition. I believe the absence of a definition could be purposeful, as God has allowed us the freedom to explore how to best relate to him. And yet, there must be certain parameters for our worship in order for us to worship rightly, in ways that honor and glorify God. Therefore, God provides guidelines for our worship throughout Scripture.

---

1. See Appendix 1 for a list of definitions of worship.

When you think of the word worship, what do you think of? Do you think of music? Or a Sunday morning church service? If those are your definitions of worship you would be right, but only partially so. Yes, music can be worship and our church services are filled with worship, but that's not all worship is. Worship is, and should be, so much more.

Did you know the Bible contains no less than six hundred references to worship? Did you know at least eighty-seven different Hebrew and Greek words are used in the pages of Scripture to describe praise and worship? Worship can be found all throughout the Bible, interwoven into the fabric of every story.

Perhaps we can begin by seeing what various words for worship mean. The word worship comes from the Anglo Saxon word *weorthscipe*, which combines two words meaning to "ascribe worth;" referring to something that shows or possesses a state of worth. In order to ascribe worth to God, we must first recognize God for who he is. Hence, worship is a response to who God is. It is a response to the being and nature of God. Praise, on the other hand, is a response to all God has done—a response to the works of God. God's actions done in, through and around his people are worthy of praise. I appreciate the way Dr. Jim Altizer differentiates between worship and praise. He says,

> . . . "praise" would be like boasting about the great things your spouse has accomplished, while "worship" would resemble appreciating your spouse because he or she is loyal, compassionate, honest and encouraging. Praise focuses on deeds, while worship focuses on character."[2]

Altizer continues,

> "Worship" centers on the character of God, while "Praise" celebrates the deeds of God. Both expressions are Biblical; both are necessary. "Worship" and "praise" are different components of the same relationship; Christians worship God for Who he is, and praise him for what he has done. Both Worship and Praise are fitting for all creatures in all situations at all times. They should be offered everywhere and in every way.[3]

It is not difficult to find biblical precedent for both praise and worship. Throughout Scripture we find numerous accounts of the people of God

2. Altizer, *The Making Of A Worship Leader*, 13.

3. Ibid., 18.

offering praise for what he has done. In 2 Samuel, chapter 22, David sang a song of deliverance recounting all God had done for him. He concluded with these words,

> For this I will praise you, oh Lord, among the nations, and sing praises to your name. (2 Sam 22:50)

Later, David encouraged the people once again to offer their praise to God because of all that had been done on their behalf,

> Oh give thanks to the Lord; call upon his name; make known his deeds among the peoples! Sing to him, sing praises to him; tell of all his wondrous works! Glory in his holy name; let the hearts of those who seek the Lord rejoice! (1 Chr 16:8–10)

The Psalms are filled with praising God for what he has done:

> Sing praises to the Lord, who sits enthroned in Zion! Tell among the peoples his deeds! (Ps 9:11)

> The Lord lives, and blessed be my rock, and exalted be the God of my salvation—the God who gave me vengeance and subdued peoples under me, who delivered me from my enemies; yes, you exalted me above those who rose against me; you rescued me from the man of violence. For this I will praise you, O Lord, among the nations, and sing to your name. (Ps 18:46–49)

> Then my tongue shall tell of your righteousness and of your praise all the day long. (Ps 35:28)

> Declare his glory among the nations, his marvelous works among all the peoples! For great is the Lord, and greatly to be praised; he is to be feared above all gods. For all the gods of the peoples are worthless idols, but the Lord made the heavens. (Ps 96:3–5)

> Sing to him, sing praises to him; tell of all his wondrous works! (Ps 105:2)

Scripture is not only filled with stories of God's people praising him for what he has done, but also with stories of how they worshiped him for Who he is. One such instance occurs at the birth of Jesus when the Magi arrived and offered their worship to the King of kings:

And going into the house they *saw the child* with Mary his mother, and they fell down and worshiped him. Then, opening their treasures, they offered him gifts, gold and frankincense and myrrh. (Matt 2:11; *emphasis* mine)

The child had not done anything for the Magi, but they bowed down and worshiped simply at the sight of the newborn King.

God is revealed in his attributes such as goodness, holiness, love, and more; and he is worshiped thusly:

When all the people of Israel saw the fire come down and the glory of the Lord on the temple, they bowed down with their faces to the ground on the pavement and worshiped and gave thanks to the Lord, saying, "For he is *good*, for his *steadfast love* endures forever." (2 Chr 7:3; *emphasis* mine)

Ascribe to the Lord, O heavenly beings, ascribe to the Lord *glory and strength.* Ascribe to the Lord the glory due his name; worship the Lord in the splendor of holiness. (Ps 29:1–2; *emphasis* mine)

Exalt the Lord our God, and worship at his holy mountain; for the Lord our God is *holy!* (Ps 99:9; *emphasis* mine)

. . . let us be grateful for receiving a kingdom that cannot be shaken, and thus let us offer to God acceptable worship, with reverence and awe, for our God is a *consuming fire.* (Heb 12:28–29; *emphasis* mine)

The word worship in the English Bible attempts to translate one of two groups of Hebrew and Greek words. The first group refers to acts of reverence while the second group consists of words that primarily refer to acts of service. Within the first group, the Hebrew word *shachah* (used 171 times[4]) means to show homage by prostrating oneself, bowing down, or stooping low. Likewise, the Greek word *proskuneo* (used 60 times[5]) means to do reverence by kneeling or lying prostrate, or to kiss towards (like kissing the ring of royalty). Within the second group, the Hebrew word *abad* (used 290 times[6]) means to serve or stand and was generally used to refer to the work of the priests and Levites as they fulfilled their worship leading

4. The NAS Old Testament Hebrew Lexicon, Strong's Number 7812
5. The NAS New Testament Greek Lexicon, Strong's Number 4352
6. The NAS Old Testament Hebrew Lexicon, Strong's Number 5647

roles in the temple. The Greek word *leitourgia* (used 6 times[7]), which is where we get the word liturgy from, refers to the service, work or ministry of worship. This is why the word liturgy is often translated "the work of the people." Liturgy is the work or action of worship done by the people during the worship "service."

Before we go much further, let me share with you the definition of worship I regularly use:

> Worship is to reflect back to God his self-revealed worth.[8]

Worship is a dialogue between God and his people. God reveals himself and humans respond accordingly. God initiates the conversation by revealing himself for Who he is and humans respond by acknowledging and reflecting the attributes of God back to him—in other words, worship. Hughes Oliphant Old says, "That God acts in history is fundamental to our theology; that we rejoice in these mighty acts is fundamental to our worship."[9]

There is an analogy involving the earth's moon and sun that reiterates this dialogical idea of revelation and response.[10] Although the moon shines brightly in the night sky, it has no light of its own. The moon simply reflects the light of the earth's sun. As worshipers, we reflect the light of the Son—Jesus Christ. Just as we see the glow of the moon reflecting the light of the sun, God sees the light of Jesus Christ, his Son, being reflected by worshipers.

A.W. Tozer states, " . . . worship originates with God and comes back to us and is reflected from us, as a mirror. God accepts no other kind of worship."[11] Robert Schaper touches on this idea of revelation and response in his definition of worship:

> Worship is the expression of a relationship in which God the Father reveals himself and his love in Christ, and by His Holy Spirit administers grace to which we respond in faith, gratitude and obedience.[12]

---

7. The NAS New Testament Greek Lexicon, Strong's Number 3009

8. Altizer, *The Making of A Worship Leader*, 14.

9. Old, *Leading in Prayer*, 237.

10. Atizer, *The Making of A Worship Leader*, 15.

11. Tozer, *Whatever Happened to Worship?*, 45.

12. Schaper, *In His Presence*, 15–16. Used by permission. All rights reserved.

First, notice that in our worship, God desires to have a relationship with us. He loves for us to be in his presence. Next, Schaper rightly mentions the revelation and response of worship. The word of God is proclaimed to the Christian community as an intentional presentation of the truth about the triune God—Father, Son, Holy Spirit—and God's relationship with his people (revelation); and there is a reply of God's people to the truth proclaimed shown by means of a prepared or spontaneous opportunity for the worshipers to answer, reply, or react (response). Our worship should be a response to what God has done, is doing and will do in our lives.

2

Whom Should We Worship?

*. . . he who is the blessed and only Sovereign, the King of kings and Lord of
lords, who alone has immortality, who dwells in unapproachable light, whom
no one has ever seen or can see. To him be honor and eternal dominion. Amen.*

1 TIMOTHY 6:15B–16

EVERYONE WORSHIPS. IT'S IN our nature to worship. Many, however, do not
worship God, but place someone or something else in his place. For some,
it may be money, relationships, career, success, or even, and possibly most
often, self. We have taken God off the throne and placed something else
in his place. In doing so, we violate the very first commandment given by
God, "You shall have no other gods besides me" (Exod 20:3). If we should
worship God and only God, we must have an accurate understanding of
who he is. Who is this God we worship? A proper view of God will allow
us to worship him fully.

First, we must understand that we worship a triune God. This trinitarian aspect of God is one of the great mysteries of our faith. Our God is one
God in three Persons—Father, Son, and Holy Spirit. James Torrance states,
"worship is . . . the gift of participating through the Spirit in the incarnate
Son's communion with the Father."[1] If God is triune, it is proper for us to
worship him thusly. Oftentimes we are very good at acknowledging one or

---

1. Torrance, *Worship, Community and the Triune God of Grace*, 20.

two Persons of the Trinity, at the expense of the other(s). To ignore any one Person of the Trinity is to neglect worshiping God to the fullest.[2]

In his plenary talk on trinitarian worship, Bruce Ware, Professor of Christian Theology at Southern Seminary in Louisville, Kentucky, shared that worship of the one true God is only rightly understood through the lens of the Trinity:

> The Father and worship—the ultimate Recipient of all praise and glory (see Eph 1:3–4, 2:18, 3:20–21, 5:20; Phil 2:9–11; Rev 5:13–14)

> The Son and worship—the direct Object of the Church's obedience and worship (see John 9:38–39, 20:28–29; Phil 2:9–11; Phil 3:3; Heb 1:6)

> The Holy Spirit and worship—the empowering Agent and indirect Object of the Church's worship (Phil 3:3)

> Trinitarian worship—all three divine Persons are together the Object of Christian worship (Matt 28:19–20; Rev 5:13–14, 5:6)[3]

Christian worship seeks to honor the Father as Christians worship the Son by the power of the Holy Spirit.

Because of trinitarian worship, early Christians were accused of polytheism. As a response to this accusation, the early church fathers defended the Christian faith and the doctrine of the Trinity.

> As if in this way also one were not All, in that All are of One, by unity (that is) of substance; while the mystery of the dispensation is still guarded, which distributes the Unity into a Trinity, placing in their order the three Persons—the Father, the Son, and the

2. When is the last time your church acknowledged all three Persons of the Trinity within a worship service? There are various ways in which to do so. Concluding a prayer in the name of the Father, Son, and Holy Spirit is very common in many church traditions. Some songs acknowledge the Trinity within their lyrics: "Holy, Holy, Holy" by Reginald Heber, "How Great Is Our God" by Chris Tomlin, Jesse Reeves and Ed Cash, and "Our God Saves" by Paul Baloche and Brenton Brown are just a few examples. Acknowledging the three in one God throughout the course of the entire service is another option. For example, use a prayer that focuses on God the Father, celebrate communion to focus on the sacrifice of Jesus Christ (the Son) and sing a song that invites the presence of the Holy Spirit. Over the course of the worship service, all three Persons of the Trinity have been acknowledged.

3. Bruce Ware "Worshiping God the Father" plenary address at WorshipGod 2014 (July 18, 2014).

Holy Ghost: three, however, not in condition, but in degree; not in substance, but in form; not in power, but in aspect; yet of one substance, and of one condition, and of one power, inasmuch as He is one God, from whom these degrees and forms and aspects are reckoned, under the name of the Father, and of the Son, and of the Holy Ghost. (Tertullian, *Against Praxeas*, 200 AD)

A man, therefore, even though he will it not, is compelled to acknowledge God the Father Almighty, and Christ Jesus the Son of God, who, being God, became man, to whom also the Father made all things subject, Himself excepted, and the Holy Spirit; and that these, therefore, are three. But if he desires to learn how it is shown still that there is one God, let him know that His power is one. As far as regards the power, therefore, God is one. But as far as regards the economy there is a threefold manifestation, as shall be proved afterwards when we give account of the true doctrine. In these things, however, which are thus set forth by us, we are at one. For there is one God in whom we must believe, but unoriginated, impassible, immortal, doing all things as He wills, in the way He wills, and when He wills. (Hippolytus, *Against The Heresy Of One Noetus*, 200 AD)

These defenses of trinitarian worship set a foundation for the writing of the Athanasian Creed,[4] commonly referred to as the "Trinitarian Creed." Used by Christian churches since the fifth century, it is the first creed in which the equality of the three persons of the Trinity is explicitly stated. The Athanasian Creed expresses two essential elements of Christian teaching: that God's Son and the Holy Spirit are of one being with the Father; and that Jesus Christ is true God and a true human being in one person. Praise be to the one God—Father, Son, and Holy Spirit.

In addition to being trinitarian, Christian worship must also have Jesus Christ at its center. Our worship must be centered on the work and life of Jesus Christ. Christian worship is made possible by Christ, and is centered upon the Christ–event—his death, burial, resurrection and ascension. Listen to the words of Paul as he describes how central Christ is to our worship:

He is the image of the invisible God, the firstborn of all creation. For by him all things were created, in heaven and on earth, visible and invisible, whether thrones or dominions or rulers or authorities—all things were created through him and for him. And he is before all things, and in him all things hold together. And he is the head of the body, the church. He is the beginning, the firstborn

4. See Appendix 2.

from the dead, that in everything he might be preeminent. For in
him all the fullness of God was pleased to dwell, and through him
to reconcile to himself all things, whether on earth or in heaven,
making peace by the blood of his cross. (Col 1:15–20)

Worship theologian Robert Webber states, "When the church worships the Father, through the Son, it praises the Father for the encompass-
ing work of the Son."[5] Christ is the center of our worship. Our worship is
designed to tell the gospel story. Webber continues,

> The gospel has to do with the creation of a good world, its falling
> away into death through sin, the assumption of the fallen creation
> through the incarnation of the Creator, the triumphant destruc-
> tion of the powers of sin and death through the death of Jesus, the
> re–creation of the creation demonstrated by His resurrection, and
> finally that anticipation of the consummation when the work of
> re-creation will be completed. In a nutshell this is the gospel of for-
> giveness, the message of substitution, and the hope of the world.
> Worship is Christocentric in that we worship the Father, in
> and through the work of the Son, by the Holy Spirit in praise and
> thanksgiving for the work of redemption. For that reason the work
> of Christ is central to Christian worship.[6]

There is no mistaking that our worship must be centered on Jesus
Christ, for Christ is the center of all things. And yet, it is not entirely un-
common for churches to make the mistake of turning their attention onto
other things. I remember one year being at a church on Father's Day. The
church had two over-sized tricycles in the sanctuary, big enough for adults
to ride. Chairs had been positioned to create a racetrack around the perim-
eter of the room and a person mimicking a game show host selected two
dads from the congregation to race around the sanctuary on the tricycles.
A digital stopwatch appeared on the large screens and loud, high–energy
music was played over the sound system. The host declared, "Ready, Set,
Go!" and the dads were off, racing around the pre–set track while the congregation cheered them on. When the first race finished, two more dads
were selected and the racing began again. Prizes were awarded to the win-
ners of the races.

This whole scenario lasted nearly twenty minutes. When asked the
purpose of the racing event, the leadership of the church responded that

5. Webber, *Worship Old and New*, 87.
6. Ibid., 91.

they wanted dads to see that church could be fun. *But what about Jesus?* This church said they were providing a worship service yet spent twenty minutes ignoring Christ. Don't get me wrong, I think we should acknowledge dads on Father's Day (and moms on Mother's Day, veterans on Veteran's Day, etc.), but a worship service is intended to turn our attention, as the gathered body of Christ, on Christ. On Father's Day, a more appropriate way to spend our time is to acknowledge dads by thanking God for placing them in our lives. We honor dads by honoring God. We should always keep the focus on God by keeping Christ at the center of our worship.

One main problem for the Church is that we become so easily distracted. We have been called to bring light to a darkened world and yet we regularly take our eyes off Jesus and allow the darkness to dim our light. Dallas Willard states,

> Churches that [produce] children of light have turned their efforts under God toward making spiritual formation in Christlikeness their primary goal. The reason most congregations fail to routinely produce children of light is distraction. While majoring in minors, they become distracted by things the New Testament says nothing about. They devote most of their thought and effort to sermons, Sunday School, style of music, denominations, camps, or board meetings. Those matters are not primary and will take care of themselves when what is primary is appropriately cared for.[7]

We must strive to keep Christ central in our worship in order to properly honor God by offering him spirit and truth worship.

Maintaining Christ as the center of our worship does not take anything away from our worship being trinitarian. The two go hand in hand. In his book, *Christ-Centered Worship*, Bryan Chapell states,

> We make our worship Christ centered not by failing to mention Father or Spirit, but by honoring them with the gospel pattern that reflects their will and purpose. We honor the Father when we sing of his greatness to humble hearts and prepare them to receive the grace that Christ provides. And were we not to mention the provision of Christ, then we would have demeaned the God who sent him no matter how much more praise we heaped upon the Father. Similarly, we honor the Spirit when we call on him to help us understand Scripture's testimony of Christ's work. And we would grieve the Spirit if we were to make him, whose ministry is

---

7. Willard and Johnson, *Renovation of the Heart in Daily Practice*, 162. Used by permission of Tyndale House Publishers, Inc. All rights reserved.

testifying of Christ, the chief object of our worship . . . We make our worship Christ-centered not by simply mentioning the name of Jesus, and definitely not by failing to honor the Father and the Spirit; we make our worship Christ-centered by shaping it to help God's people understand and appreciate the grace in all Scripture that culminates in their Savior's ministry.[8]

Even elements of the worship service that do not directly mention the name of Jesus should be shaped by his redemptive work as our worship possesses the central theme of celebrating Christus Victor—the victorious Christ; all the while honoring the Father and the Spirit. As we participate in Christ-centered worship, we join in the acclamation—Christ has died, Christ is risen, Christ will come again!

8. Chapell, *Christ-Centered Worship*, 114–115.

3

Where Should We Worship?

*You may worship God anywhere, at any time, but the chances are that you will
not do so unless you have first learned to worship Him somewhere in some
particular place, at some particular time.*

THEODORE ROOSEVELT

THE BIBLE MAKES IT clear that God is everywhere. There is nowhere we can
go, whether on earth or beyond the galaxies, to escape the presence of God.
The psalmist makes this clear when he cries out:

> Where can I go from your Spirit? Where can I flee from your pres-
> ence? If I go up to the heavens, you are there. If I make my bed in
> the depths, you are there. If I rise on the wings of the dawn, if I
> settle on the far side of the sea, even there your hand will guide me,
> your right hand will hold me fast. (Ps 139:7–10)

Theologians call this omnipresence; being everywhere at once. And though
God is omnipresent, the Bible also teaches that God is present in a special
way in specific locations.

The Altar

When early Old Testament followers of Yahweh wanted to worship God,
or when a person encountered God in a special way, they would build an

altar as a place to worship. The first recorded place we find an altar is with Cain and Abel. We don't find the word altar in the text, but it says that they brought their sacrifices before the Lord:

> In the course of time Cain brought to the Lord an offering of the fruit of the ground, and Abel also brought of the firstborn of his flock and of their fat portions. (Gen 4:3–4)

In order to offer their sacrifices to God, Cain and Abel had to bring their offerings somewhere, and offerings were done at altars.

Following the flood, we read of Noah building an altar to offer worship to the Lord:

> Then Noah built an altar to the Lord and took some of every clean animal and some of every clean bird and offered burnt offerings on the altar. (Gen 8:20)

In Genesis 12, we read of Abraham, the father of nations, building the first of many altars:

> Then the Lord appeared to Abram and said, "To your offspring I will give this land." So he built there an altar to the Lord, who had appeared to him. (Gen 12:7)

In Genesis 35 Jacob builds an altar out of obedience to God:

> God said to Jacob, "Arise, go up to Bethel and dwell there. Make an altar there to the God who appeared to you when you fled from your brother Esau." So Jacob said to his household and to all who were with him, "Put away the foreign gods that are among you and purify yourselves and change your garments. Then let us arise and go up to Bethel, so that I may make there an altar to the God who answers me in the day of my distress and has been with me wherever I have gone." . . . Then God went up from him in the place where he had spoken with him. And Jacob set up a pillar in the place where he had spoken with him, a pillar of stone. He poured out a drink offering on it and poured oil on it. So Jacob called the name of the place where God had spoken with him Bethel. (Gen 35:1–3, 13–15)

From the beginning of the story of God, worshipers would offer their worship by means of the altar.

The Tabernacle

At Mount Sinai, following the exodus out of Egypt, the people of God became the nation of God. As a nation, Israel needed a place to come into the presence of God to offer sacrifice and worship. Small altars would no longer be enough; something larger was needed. So, on Sinai, God told Moses, "I want the people of Israel to build me a sacred residence where I can live among them" (Exod 25:8).

It's important to note that it was God who initiated the building of the tabernacle, and not Moses. God not only told Moses to build it, but he gave him very specific instructions to follow: "You must make this tabernacle and its furnishings exactly according to the plans I will show you" (Exod 25:9).

God does not leave it to human beings to define the type of worship they offer. It is God who decides what is good, pleasing and acceptable worship—not us. God knew what was best and he told Moses in detail. We see that God initiating worship is of great significance as the whole second half of Exodus is dedicated to the details of the tabernacle. From Exodus 25:10–30:38, God gives instructions to Moses on how to build the sanctuary. In 31:1–11, God appoints two men, Bezalel and Oholiab, to be the leaders of the building project, the general contractors, and provides for them the wisdom needed to complete the task. The last chapters of Exodus describe the fulfillment of the instructions, in detail. It is here that we find that the tabernacle ended up exactly the way the Lord instructed.

Now, according to God's plan, the tabernacle replaces the altar as the primary location where God reveals his presence to his people. But as God so often does, he does not eliminate the old way of worship. He incorporates the altar into the tabernacle.[1]

When we read Exodus we can't help but see the importance of the tabernacle. Of the three important topics of the entire book—the other two being the Exodus and the law—the vast majority of the book deals with the tabernacle.

The author of the book of Hebrews informs us why God was so concerned that Moses followed his instructions to the letter as the Israelites built the tabernacle and its contents:

1. It is important to note that God seldom eliminates one form of worship when introducing a new one. Just as God incorporated the altar in with the tabernacle, so we as worship leaders should consider incorporating older forms of worship in with newer forms (i.e. hymns and praise choruses, responsive readings and readers theater, drama skits and video, etc.).

> They serve in a place of worship that is only a copy, a shadow of the real one in heaven. For when Moses was getting ready to build the Tabernacle, God gave him this warning: "Be sure that you make everything according to the design I have shown you here on the mountain." (Heb 8:5)

The reason such care had to be taken with the construction of the tabernacle is that its very structure and the material out of which it was built served as a reflection of heaven.

As we've seen, during Old Testament times the faithful would go to certain locations in order to meet with God in worship. The tabernacle was such a place, and the symbolism of the entire structure revolved around one central idea: the Holy God was present in the midst of the camp.

The tabernacle complex had three parts, dividing the larger wandering camp of Israelites into four parts. These included the holiest place (Holy of Holies), which was separated by a thick curtain from the Holy Place, where only the priests and Levites (the worship leaders) could enter. There was also the courtyard where the sacrifices would take place and the Israelite camp proper where all ritually clean Israelites could be. To complete the picture, there was the area outside the camp where Gentiles and the ritually unclean would be—the rest of the world, so to speak.

The tabernacle was to be placed in the center of camp, surrounded by the tribes of Israel. In this way, God's tent, the tabernacle, was like the tent of any ancient monarch—in the center surrounded by his people.

The tabernacle housed key liturgical centers, or pieces, to accommodate worship. These pieces were symbolic representations of God's presence here on earth. They also served functional purposes for worship. Just as the altar found its way into the tabernacle, each of the five liturgical pieces from the tabernacle—the ark of the covenant, the lampstand, the table of the bread of the presence, the sacrificial altar and the altar of incense—end up in the Temple that Solomon builds later in the Old Testament.[2]

---

2. A complete study on the tabernacle is beyond the scope of this book. A brief look at the liturgical pieces found in the tabernacle shows us: 1) The Ark of the Covenant—the earthly symbol of heaven which contained, among other items, the tablets of the covenant. The ark was connected to the covenant as a concrete token of the divine presence; 2) The Lampstand—According to Leviticus 24, the Lampstand was to be kept lit at all times serving as a reminder that God was making his presence known; 3) The Table of the Bread of Presence—built for the purpose of holding the bread of the Presence representing the presence of God with his people. The 12 loaves represented the 12 tribes of Israel; 4) The Sacrificial Altar—located just in front of the tabernacle, but within the courtyard. The purpose of the sacrificial altar was just as it sounds—for offering burnt

When we look at the Old Testament tabernacle, we could easily have the tendency to think about it as an institution focused on endless sacrifices and tedious rituals. But this dismisses its significance in the Old Testament and even the purpose of Christ's coming. The tabernacle was a symbol of a higher reality—heaven here on earth. It was truly the means by which God and his people "connected." Just as we find God in Christ, the people of Israel found God in his tabernacle.

The tabernacle was God's home on earth. It symbolically represented heaven on earth. When we view the tabernacle in terms of God's presence, it becomes obvious how Jesus, our Immanuel ("God With Us"), fulfills the role the tabernacle played in the time of Moses and David. Most English translations of John 1:14 provide a rather bland rendition of this passage:

> The Word became flesh and made his dwelling among us. We have
> seen his glory, the glory of the One and only, who came from the
> Father, full of grace and truth. (John 1:14)

But the passage comes alive when we realize that the verb translated "dwelled" or "lived" (*eskenosen*) is formed from the noun "tabernacle" (*skene*). We feel the impact of this verse when we translate it as "the Word . . . tabernacled among us." Jesus is our tabernacle! Where he is, there is God. When someone met Jesus, he or she was in the presence of God.

The Temple

King David longed to build a formal place of worship for the people to gather and worship the Lord. He fervently sought the Lord, but God told him that it was David's son, Solomon, who would build the temple:

> He said to me, 'It is Solomon your son who shall build my house
> and my courts, for I have chosen him to be my son, and I will be
> his father. (1 Chr 28:6)

---

sacrifices; 5) The Altar of Incense—this altar had one very practical purpose. With all the slaughtering of sacrifices, the odor would have been overpowering without incense. The sweet smell of incense was pleasing to the Lord, and twice a day the priests were to light the incense burners.

There are many other aspects of the tabernacle that are beyond the scope of this book: the oil for the lampstand, the priestly garments, the consecration of the priests, atonement money, the basin for washing, and the anointing oil and incense. For further study on the Tabernacle, I would recommend *Life Principles for Worship from the Tabernacle* by W. Barber/E. Rasnake/R. Shepherd, *The Tabernacle: Its Priests and Its Services* by William Brown, and *Enter His Courts with Praise!* by Andrew Hill.

During this time, Israel was set in the middle of pagan nations and peoples—people who had temples and rituals that represented their gods. The reason that God wanted a permanent home, a house of worship among His people, was that he wanted a place where his acts would be remembered.

Worship is remembrance. We remember God's acts of mercy and salvation through the word and sacred actions that proclaim and enact God's acts of salvation. And we generally do this in a particular place—the church building, the house where God's people gather.

I am persuaded that God does not have a problem with form. It is, after all, God who created form. Moreover, God became form through the Incarnation. It is in the form of a man, Jesus Christ, which the world sees and knows God. God encountered humankind in the most profound way through the Incarnation.

We find this principle of Incarnation foreshadowed in the temple. In the temple, God resided and met with His people through symbols and rituals. Through these visible, tangible, concrete signs, the families of Israel approached the "throne" to worship God.

Unfortunately, Israel often got too invested in the form through which God's acts of salvation were presented. This is what Stephen, echoing the prophets, reprimanded Israel for when they accused him of blasphemy (see Acts 7:47–49). Today, we have the potential of facing the same problem. We can become overly invested in the house of worship (the building) and in its furniture (the form of worship) that we forget the One these forms are pointing to. Of course, there is nothing wrong with form; it is form for the sake of form that we need to avoid.

Solomon started building the temple four years after he became king. Construction of the temple was completed after seven years. Only the finest wood and materials were used to build the temple. And only the best craftsmen were selected to work on the project.

After the temple was built, Solomon asked the priests to come and dedicate the temple to God. The priests brought the Ark of the Covenant and placed it in the temple. Once again we see God incorporating the old way of worship in with the new. When the Ark was placed in the temple, a large cloud filled the temple and Solomon rejoiced that God's presence was in their midst. They praised the Lord, thanking him for keeping his covenant with his people and a big celebration began that lasted fourteen days. It was a time to thank God and joyfully praise him.

The temple was rectangular and had various areas that served different purposes for worship. The first area was a gathering space, also called the porch. This served as an entrance to the temple.

According to Scripture, two courts surrounded the temple. The Inner Court, or Court of the Priests, contained the Altar of Burnt Offering and several lavers (wash basins). It is here where cleansing and sacrifices would take place. The Outer Court, also called the Great Court, is where the people assembled for worship.

The Holy of Holies was an incredibly important worship space as it held the Ark of the Covenant, God's throne on earth. This most holy place was decorated with the finest wood (cedars of Lebanon—1 Kgs 6:16) and overlaid with gold (1 Kgs 6:20, 21, 30). The room contained two large cherubim, a large wooden door, a thick veil, and no windows. Just as with the tabernacle, color scheme was symbolic. The veil was blue, which represented the heavens and red, or crimson, which represented the earth. The purple elements, a combination of the two colors, represented a meeting of the heavens and the earth.

Needless to say, the temple of God built by Solomon was an incredible building project. In the sixth century, Solomon's temple was included on a list of seven wonders complied by Gregory, Bishop of Tours. The list included the Pharos (lighthouse) of Alexandria and Noah's Ark. Even Sir Isaac Newton, the noted English scientist, mathematician and theologian, was so intrigued by the temple of Solomon that he studied and wrote extensively on the temple, dedicating an entire chapter of *The Chronology of Ancient Kingdoms* to his observations on the design and geometry of the temple. And none of this should surprise us, for after all, it was God who designed every detail of the temple.

In addition to Jesus becoming our tabernacle, as seen earlier, he also identified himself with the Temple. John Piper states,

> Jesus identified himself as the true temple. "Something greater than the temple is here." In himself he would fulfill everything the temple stood for, especially the "place" where believers meet God. He diverted attention away from worship as a localized activity with outward forms and pointed toward a personal, spiritual experience with himself at the center. Worship does not have to have a building, a priesthood, and a sacrificial system. It has to have the risen Jesus.[3]

3. Piper, *Let the Nations Be Glad*, 217.

The Whole Earth

The pages of Scripture are filled with phrases declaring that the whole earth offers praise and worship to the Lord.

> All the earth worships you and sings praises to you; they sing praises to your name. (Ps 66:4)

> Sing praises to the Lord, for he has done gloriously; let this be made known in all the earth. (Isa 12:5)

> For you shall go out in joy and be led forth in peace; the mountains and the hills before you shall break forth into singing, and all the trees of the field shall clap their hands. (Isa 55:12)

God is not only worthy of praise but will receive praise regardless of our actions. The praise of God cannot be silenced or stifled. And if humans refuse to praise or are unable to praise, then creation will pick up the slack:

> And some of the Pharisees in the crowd said to him, "Teacher, rebuke your disciples." He answered, "I tell you, if these were silent, the very stones would cry out." (Luke 19:39–41)

We have the opportunity and privilege to worship the Creator amidst and throughout his creation. As we worship, we join with the trees clapping, the rocks crying, the waves exclaiming, and the fields declaring the praises of God.

The Throne

The Bible speaks of heaven as a place where God's presence is uniquely present:

> For Christ has entered, not into holy places made with hands, which are copies of the true things, but into heaven itself, now to appear in the presence of God on our behalf. (Heb 9:24)

> And now, Father, glorify me in your own presence with the glory that I had with you before the world existed. (John 17:5)

Wayne Grudem states,

> We might find it misleading to say that God is "more present" in heaven than anywhere else, but it would not be misleading to say

that God is present in a special way in heaven, present especially there to bless and to show forth his glory. We could also say that God manifests his presence more fully in heaven than elsewhere.[4]

As we worship here on earth we are being prepared for an eternity of worshiping the Father around the throne. As we worship here and now, we join with creation, in heaven and earth, in responding to who God is and what he has done.

> Then I looked, and I heard around the throne and the living creatures and the elders the voice of many angels, numbering myriads of myriads and thousands of thousands, saying with a loud voice,
>
> "Worthy is the Lamb who was slain,
> to receive power and wealth and wisdom and might
> and honor and glory and blessing!"
>
> And I heard every creature in heaven and on earth and under the earth and in the sea, and all that is in them, saying,
>
> "To him who sits on the throne and to the Lamb
> be blessing and honor and glory and might forever and ever!"
> And the four living creatures said, "Amen!" and the elders fell down and worshiped. (Rev 5:11–14)

Oh Lord, may it be on earth as it is in heaven.

No matter where we go, it is right to join with all creation praising God and offering him our worship. There is no need to wait until we arrive at a certain location, as worship should not be relegated to any particular spot. The right location to worship God is exactly where you are.

Though there is no specific place in which worship is more acceptable than another, I hope we have seen that places are beneficial to our patterns of worship. I like the quote attributed to Theodore Roosevelt at the beginning of this chapter, "You may worship God anywhere, at any time, but the chances are that you will not do so unless you have first learned to worship Him somewhere in some particular place, at some particular time." God has established certain locations as special meeting places. Today those meeting places include church facilities as well as other places of worship. But God does not intend for our worship to only be contained within those spaces. God desires for us to worship him in all places and at all times.

---

4. Grudem, *Systematic Theology*, 176.

4

Why Worship?

There are two ways, one of life and one of death, but a great difference between the two ways. The way of life, then, is this: first, you shall love God who made you; second, love your neighbor as yourself, and do not do to another what you would not want done to you.

DIDACHE, CHAPTER 1

IT IS ONE THING to understand worship and another to believe we should worship. If we are to worship God we must consider why we should even worship at all.

It's What We Were Created For

There is not a people group anywhere in the world that does not have some kind of religion and basic desire to worship. Human beings have a natural bent toward worshiping God. The problem is that we get confused as to whom we should be worshiping.

From the very beginning of time, God instilled within creation the desire to worship him. The Psalmist shows us that all creation is capable of worshiping the Lord—the heavens, the earth and all its inhabitants (animate and inanimate); the sun, moon, and stars are all called upon to praise the Lord (see Ps 148). As Christ followers, our worship is a natural expression of who we are in Christ. The Westminster Catechism states, "The chief end of man is to glorify God and enjoy him forever." John Piper expresses it this way, "The deepest longing of the human heart is to know and enjoy the glory of God. We were made for this."[1] It is in our being to worship God.

I understand this concept is difficult to grasp. It's hard to look around at all that is going on in our world today and think that our natural inclination is to worship God—after all, our culture's moral compass is nearly non-existent. But human beings were created to worship the Creator. Before the fall, it was natural for Adam and Eve to worship God. It is because of sin that we struggle with the idea that we were made to worship God. We call it a sin nature, but based on God's plan and design, sin is far from natural and does its best to prevent us from worshiping God to the fullest. A.W. Tozer states, "All of the examples that we have in the Bible illustrate that glad and devoted and reverent worship is the normal employment of moral beings."[2]

Praise and worship are a part of our spiritual make-up. We were created, not only with the desire, but also with the capacity to acknowledge God through praise and worship. From the very beginning of our life, God expects us to respond to him in worship. The psalmist affirms that even from birth we have been ordained to declare the praises of God:

> O Lord, our Lord, how majestic is your name in all the earth! You have set your glory above the heavens. From the lips of children and infants you have ordained praise because of your enemies, to silence the foe and the avenger. (Ps 8:1–2; NIV)

We were created to worship and enjoy him forever.

To Rehearse God's Story

Throughout Scripture, the people of God actively remembered all God had done for them and their ancestors. Rehearsing God's story reminds us of who God is and what he has done for us. The grand narrative of God's actions throughout history includes creation (God created all things seen and unseen); incarnation (God sent his one and only Son to redeem his fallen creation); and re-creation (God will make all things new again). This is the story of God, from Genesis to Revelation. As we worship, we must participate in rehearsing the grand story of God. Robert Webber states,

1. Piper, *Seeing and Savoring Jesus Christ*, 14.
2. Tozer, *Whatever Happened to Worship?*, 13.

Worship does truth. It tells and enacts God's story—how God rescues creatures and creation. . . . Sunday worship, every Sunday, is a celebration of God's story. And the constant bathing of our worship in this story—songs, preaching, baptism, Eucharist, and the Christian-year celebrations—form and shape our conscious and unconscious living in this theatre of God's glory![3]

The Hebrew people knew the importance of remembering God's saving actions. All throughout the Old Testament we see the people of God worshiping him by means of remembering all of God's acts. The people of God celebrated an annual festival to remember how God had delivered them from the hand of Pharaoh in Egypt. This feast called Passover is still celebrated today. God even instructed Moses to keep the Lord's mighty deeds fresh in the minds of future generations:

> When your son asks you in time to come, "What is the meaning of the testimonies and the statutes and the rules that the Lord our God has commanded you?" Then you shall say to your son, "We were Pharaoh's slaves in Egypt. And the Lord brought us out of Egypt with a mighty hand. And the Lord showed signs and wonders, great and grievous, against Egypt and against Pharaoh and all his household, before our eyes. And he brought us out from there, that he might bring us in and give us the land that he swore to give to our fathers. And the Lord commanded us to do all these statutes, to fear the Lord our God, for our good always, that he might preserve us alive, as we are this day. And it will be righteousness for us, if we are careful to do all this commandment before the Lord our God, as he has commanded us." (Deut 6:20–25)

The Lord instructed Moses to teach the future generations the story of God. And he did. Throughout the New Testament, Moses' descendants continued to remember all God accomplished, including the culmination of God's works in Jesus Christ. Peter and John recalled the story of God after they healed a lame man at the Gate Beautiful (Acts 3:17–26). Stephen, as his accusers held stones in their hands, walked his "audience" through the story of God from Abraham to Jesus Christ (Acts 7:2–53). And what a speech that was!

The Apostle Peter reminds us of why it is important to recall God's story:

3. Webber, *Ancient-Future Time*, 171.

> But you are a chosen race, a royal priesthood, a holy nation, a people for his own possession, that you may proclaim the excellencies of him who called you out of darkness into his marvelous light. Once you were not a people, but now you are God's people; once you had not received mercy, but now you have received mercy. (1 Pet 2:9–10)

John Witvliet, Director of the Calvin Institute for Christian Worship, states that "one criterion to apply to worship in any congregation, regardless of the liturgical style it embraces, is that of historical remembrance and proclamation: Does worship proclaim the whole sweep of divine activity past, present, and future?"[4] Rehearsing God's story of creation, incarnation and re-creation keeps us focused on what's important—Jesus, the Christ, the Son of the living God.

To Celebrate God

The essence of worship is the celebration of God. Our faith develops when it is expressed in celebration. Good celebrations can foster and nourish faith. Poor celebrations have the potential of weakening our faith. We find encouragement for faith building celebratory worship throughout the book of Psalms. Psalm 100 offers us an exemplary model of how we should worship as we gather:

> Shout for joy to the Lord, all the earth.
> Worship the Lord with gladness;
> come before him with joyful songs.
> Know that the Lord is God.
> It is he who made us, and we are his;
> we are his people, the sheep of his pasture.
> Enter his gates with thanksgiving
> and his courts with praise;
> give thanks to him and praise his name.
> For the Lord is good and his love endures forever;
> his faithfulness continues through all generations. (NIV)

Celebration is an appropriate aspect of worship because of the joy given by God found in Christ. Our worship should be filled with joy because of who God is and what he has done for us. Think about what God did through Christ on your behalf. Is this not reason to celebrate?

4. Witvliet, *Worship Seeking Understanding*, 36.

Throughout Scripture we see that celebratory worship is closely connected to feasting. Even today it is common to celebrate around food—birthday parties, anniversary dinners, picnics, church potlucks, etc.

In the Old Testament, we find many examples of worship and feasting being connected. When the people of God wanted to remember (worship) what God had done for them, they would do so by means of a feast, or festival.[5] The major festivals of Old Testament Israel were, in calendar order, Passover, the Feast of Unleavened Bread, Firstfruits, the Feast of Weeks (Pentecost), the Feast of Trumpets, the Day of Atonement, and the Feast of Booths (or Tabernacles). A feast is an appropriate way to celebrate.

Jesus knew the importance of food. Much of Jesus' ministry was done around, or in the presence of, food. Furthermore, the Lord incorporates a feast into our regular times of worship by means of the Eucharist.[6] This time of thanksgiving is appropriately considered a *celebration* of communion.

I appreciate Ronald Allen and Gordon Borror's perspective on the celebratory nature of worship:

> As a thoughtful gift is a celebration of a birthday, as a special evening out is a celebration of an anniversary, as a warm eulogy is a celebration of a life, as a sexual embrace is a celebration of a marriage—so worship is a celebration of God.[7]

Worship that celebrates God takes effort. It is easy to go to church; that is mere attendance. It is much more difficult to celebrate because celebration requires participation and energy. Nevertheless, celebrating God is worth any effort it takes on our part because God is worthy of all praise and worship and deserves to be celebrated in ways that honor and magnify his holy name. True worship is a joyous celebration of the life, death, and resurrection of Jesus Christ.

To Join In An Eternal Effort

I have often said that as a Worship Pastor, I have the best job in the world. I get to lead people in what we will be doing for all eternity—worshiping

5. Many of the Old Testament festivals were established by God as a way for the people to remember what he had done for them. People's memories are fickle so God wanted to set forth specific opportunities for the people to remember by means of their worship.

6. Eucharist is Greek for "thanksgiving." Other terms used in Scripture for the Eucharist include the Lord's Supper, the breaking of bread, and communion.

7. Allen and Borror, *Worship: Rediscovering the Missing Jewel*, 19.

God. Throughout Scripture we see that the worship of God is an eternal effort that will ultimately be performed by all of creation. Although many deny him worship on this side of eternity, there will come a time when everyone and everything will offer God the glory he is due.

> All mankind will fear; they will proclaim the works of God and ponder what he has done. (Psalm 64:9)

> All the nations you have made will come and worship before you, O Lord; they will bring glory to your name. For you are great and do marvelous deeds; you alone are God. (Ps 86:9–10)

> At the name of Jesus every knee should bow, in heaven and on earth and under the earth, and every tongue confess that Jesus Christ is Lord, to the glory of God the Father. (Phil 2:10–11)

When we worship we join with the angels and heavenly host praising God and saying, "Glory to God in the highest" (Luke 2:14); "Holy, holy, holy, is the Lord God Almighty, who was and is and is to come" (Rev 4:8); "Worthy is the Lamb who was slain, to receive power and wealth and wisdom and might and honor and glory and blessing" (Rev 5:12).

God Wants to Form Us Spiritually

There's a saying, "We are what we eat"? Dieticians use this phrase to reiterate the truth that what goes into our bodies will either help develop our physical being or hinder our growth development. A diet of candy and sugary treats will surely taste good at the time, but does not have much nutritional value and will not do well for building muscles and maintaining a healthy body. In fact, this kind of diet will have the opposite effect and potentially damage our body. The adage "we are what we eat" is true for our spiritual lives as well. What goes in, shapes our soul.

My mom used to say, "Garbage in, garbage out." The things we see and hear, that which we put into our minds and lives, will eventually come out of our mouths and will be represented by the way we live. The question is, "What will we put in?" Our spiritual nourishment is a direct result of our spiritual food intake. Putting in spiritually healthy food builds spiritual muscles and wards off spiritual diseases. So the question is: as leaders in worship, what will we put into Christ's body—the gathered fellowship of worshipers?

45

As we gather as a community of faith in the presence of God, we gather with the expectation that our worship will form us in spiritual ways. Worshiping God through the various elements of a worship service should lead to the spiritual formation of our lives. Isaiah 29:13 tells us, "The Lord says: 'These people come near to me with their mouth and honor me with their lips, but their hearts are far from me. Their worship of me is made up only of rules taught by men.'" The elements of a worship service should not merely be rituals that we perform in order to appease God. Each element should be an act of worship offered to God, and as such serve to form us spiritually.

The following is a brief look at each worship element in light of spiritual formation.

Music

The songs in our worship services are to a great degree formative. The songs we sing in church lodge themselves into our minds as truth. As the worshiper sings truth found within the songs, their faith is strengthened, their theology is founded and their spirit is formed. John Wesley says,

> Above all, sing spiritually. Have an eye to God in every word you sing. Aim at pleasing him more than yourself, or any other creature. In order to do this attend strictly to the sense of what you sing, and see that your heart is not carried away with the sound, but offered to God continually; so shall your singing be such as the Lord will approve here, and reward you when he cometh in the clouds of heaven.[8]

Prayer

It has been said, worship prays God's story. As a result of Christ's redeeming work, public prayer ushers all of creation to the Father through Jesus Christ by the Holy Spirit. As we pray we join with God on the journey of Him changing us from the inside out by the power of Christ working within. Our prayers shape that which we are, both on the inside and on the outside.

---

8. From Sacred Melody, 1761, quoted in preface to *The Methodist Hymnal* (1964), viii. See Appendix 10 for the complete list of "Directions for Singing" by John Wesley.

Scripture Reading

The use of Scripture is foundational in celebrating God in worship. The Bible has always been central to the life of the Christian church. The ancient Hebrew stories and songs that permeated the Jewish world of Jesus' day profoundly shaped even Jesus himself as he lived on the earth. The earliest Christians searched the Scriptures in an attempt to understand what Almighty God had accomplished through Jesus, and as a result, their lives were shaped accordingly. Today, we continue to study the Scriptures to discover how to live and thus, how to worship.

Communion

Our time of worship at the Table should leave us changed. When we enter the presence of God, our hearts should burn within us as we remember that the one who was crucified, dead, buried, and rose again, is now alive and within us. This leads the worshiper to the mysterious greatness of God found at the Table. I believe participating in communion on a regular basis is biblical (see Acts 20:7, 1 Cor 11:25) and vital to our spiritual growth. As we participate in the breaking of the bread and the drinking of the cup, we are drawn closer to Christ.

Sermon

The ministry of proclaiming the word of God through the preaching of a sermon must be approached as an act of worship. The purpose of the word of God is to reveal the Word of God (Jesus Christ). In Scripture, the people who saw God were never quite the same again. Their lives were transformed. So should it be every worship service in which the Word is proclaimed.

Silence

Silence has long been an important aspect of personal and corporate worship. It is a time to quiet the soul in order to become receptive to God's revelation. Embracing times of silence in worship allows God the opportunity to speak. Much of what else we do in worship is directed toward God. In every element of worship, there should be aspects of revelation and response, yet silence is primarily the time to allow God to be the communicator as we do nothing else but listen to his voice. As we hear from God we open ourselves to the opportunity to be transformed by the renewing of our minds. In silence, God is given permission to form us from within in a way that only he can.[9]

Giving

It is within forms of giving which the disciple of Jesus experiences a renewed and transformed life, becoming as the very nature of Jesus Christ, whom himself gave his life as an act of worship to the Father.

Baptism

In baptism we find our identity and are incorporated into Christ's life and his body—the Church. Through baptism, God draws us near to himself. For those who have previously been baptized and are observing someone else's baptism, the worshiper should remember their own baptism allowing God to refresh the sign and seal of regeneration upon their own lives. Spiritual formation through baptism should continue to occur instead of being a one–time occurrence.

God desires for spiritual formation to occur any time, any place, and in every way. Each element of worship within the worship service should lead the worshiper to be:

> . . . transformed by the renewing of your mind, that you may prove what is that good and acceptable and perfect will of God. (Rom 12:2)

As we worship God, we are spiritually formed into the likeness of Christ.

Jesus Tells Us To Worship

The most important reason we should worship is because Jesus tells us to. When Jesus was challenged regarding the most important command to follow, he replied: worship (see Mark 12:28–30). First and foremost, followers

9. We will further discuss silence as an act of worship in chapter 10.

of Christ are to worship God with complete abandon. Worship is the most important function of any believer and we must worship with everything we have.

Of course, the second command adds on to the first: to evangelize, fellowship, and care for others as an overflow of our worship (see Mark 12:31). As we worship, we are drawing near to God and becoming increasingly like his Son. As we become more like Jesus, we will, as a result, begin to act like Jesus. How did Jesus act? He loved others and proclaimed the good news of salvation. Furthermore, loving God and loving others means submitting to the Father's will just as Jesus submitted to his will (see Luke 22:42).

Jesus' own life provides an example for us to follow. Worship must be our first priority because it draws us near to God. All other functions of the Church are a natural result of our worship.

The Purpose of the Gathering

I feel I would be remiss at this point if I did not consider the struggle between worship and evangelism within our churches. Over the past few decades, there has been a movement in the United States to convert the Sunday worship service into an evangelistic gathering. Historically, however, Christians gathered for worship and scattered for evangelism. The worship service has never been intended to be an evangelistic event. This makes sense as only those who believe in God can worship God. It may sound obvious, but those who do not know God cannot worship the God they do not know. In fact, Scripture calls those who do not know God, enemies of God (see Rom 5:10; Col 1:21; Jas 4:4). The worship of God is the priority and ultimate culmination of his redemptive work. Though important, evangelism is not the primary purpose of the gathering (see 1 Cor 14).

It seems that Christians today have turned evangelism into inviting people to church rather than sharing the gospel of Jesus Christ. Marva Dawn states:

> Worship is the language of love and growth between believers and God; evangelism is the language of introduction between those who believe and those who don't. To confuse the two and put on worship the burden of evangelism robs the people of God of their responsibility to care about the neighbor, defrauds the believers of

transforming depth, and steals from God the profound praise of
which he is worthy.[10]

Nowhere in Scripture do we find, "Worship the Lord to win over unbelievers." Instead, we find countless passages that encourage us to worship God
because he is worthy of our worship. I agree with James McDonald when
he states,

> The problem in the church today is that we treat God's glory as a
> by-product and the missional activities of the church as the pri-
> mary thing when the opposite is what Scripture demands.

Historically, Sunday worship expresses three truths: It remembers the story
of God and his saving action in history; it experiences the renewing presence of God; and it anticipates the completion of God's work in the new
heavens and the new earth. The worship of God is a supernatural experience as mortals commune with the Immortal. Pastor Matt Chandler states:

> Worship gatherings are not always spectacular, but they are always
> supernatural. And if a church looks for or works for the spectacu-
> lar, she may miss the supernatural. If a person enters a gathering
> to be wowed with something impressive, with a style that fits him
> just right, with an order of service and song selection designed just
> the right way, that person may miss the supernatural presence of
> God. Worship is supernatural whenever people come hungry to
> respond, react, and receive from God for who He is and what He
> has done. A church worshipping as a Creature of the Word doesn't
> show up to perform or be entertained; she comes desperate and
> needy, thirsty for grace, receiving from the Lord and the body of
> Christ, and then gratefully receiving what she needs as she offers
> her praise—the only proper response to the God who saves us.[11]

Our worship services must be a place where we expect something supernatural to occur as we meet with, magnify, and exalt Almighty God. Oftentimes, however, we have turned our worship services into evangelistic
meetings with the intent to wow unbelievers into the kingdom.

There are some concerned that evangelism will somehow get lost if the
Church focuses primarily on worship. Dawn would counter that,

> In a culture just as pagan and anti-Christian as ours (both Ro-
> mans/Greeks and Jews were opposed to this "Jesus movement"),

10. Dawn, *A Royal "Waste" Of Time*, 124.
11. Chandler, *Creature of the Word*, 42.

the early Christians did not try to figure out how to attract their neighbors. They did not try to control the process. Instead, they simply practiced Churchbeing,[12] so that the Lord could do his work of adding new believers.[13]

Now don't get me wrong; I am not minimizing the church's responsibility of sharing the gospel of Jesus Christ. I am a firm believer in evangelism. There are people all around us—family, friends, co-workers—that are on their way to an eternity without Christ because they have not yet heard of, or have rejected, God's grace. This should break our hearts and compel us toward evangelism. But we must not confuse the purpose of our worship gatherings as times for evangelism. As John Piper states at the beginning of his book "Let the Nations Be Glad,"

> Missions is not the ultimate goal of the church. Worship is. Missions exists because worship doesn't. Worship is ultimate, not missions, because God is ultimate, not man. When this age is over, and the countless millions of the redeemed fall on their faces before the throne of God, missions will be no more. It is a temporal necessity. But worship abides forever.[14]

This is not to say that we must wait on loving others until we have figured out how to love God properly. Returning to Jesus' Great Commandment found in Mark 12, following the two commands does not encourage the neglect of one command over the other. Our primary calling in life is to worship God. As we worship we are compelled to love others and share God's love with them. It is clear, therefore, that as we obey the first command we become better at obeying the second. By obeying the second command we are compelled to further obedience of the first command. We must realize that there is an important connection between worship and evangelism:

> Of course the distinction is not total, for if believers worship with gladness and passion, anyone not yet a part of the community certainly will be attracted to the One who is the object of their worship. But to focus the worship on evangelistic introduction

12. Dawn recommends using the word Churchbeing because words like *community* and *church* are misused, overused, abused, and confused. "It is crucial," Dawn states, "that churches ask fundamental questions about who we are as Church and how we practice being Church in our worship life" (Dawn, *A Royal "Waste" of Time*, 103).

13. Dawn, *A Royal "Waste" Of Time*, 131.

14. Piper, *Let the Nations Be Glad*, 17.

deprives believers of deeper nurturing toward Churchbeing and deprives God of the intimate and involved worship due him from the Church.[15]

A.W. Tozer states that "practically every great deed done in the church of Christ all the way back to the apostle Paul was done by people blazing with the radiant worship of their God."[16] This would include sharing the good news of Jesus Christ with the world. It is through our worship that we are set ablaze to shine the light of Christ in a darkened world. As Dawn states,

> To be the sort of people who will gladly fulfill our responsibility for witness and mentoring and nurturing care we need meaty worship—worship that engages us deeply in an encounter with the God whose splendor is illimitably beyond our understanding, worship that shakes us out of our narcissism and consumerism, worship that disciplines us and thereby equips us for the work of the kingdom in witness and vocation and suffering.[17]

Reformer John Calvin believed that "Christian worship both testifies to the goodness of God before the world and is an act of separation, signaling a clear delineation between the world and the worshiping community."[18]

One other item to consider, before moving on, is the neglect of the corporate worship gathering in lieu of other activities, often for the sake of evangelism. I have heard of churches doing "Gone Serving" Sundays where they send their congregation out into the community to pick up litter or paint park benches, i.e. community service, in lieu of gathering together for a worship service. This is admirable, but potentially a dangerous misuse of the Sunday morning meeting time. As spiritual leaders, our desire should be that our congregation would be spiritually formed during the worship service so much so that their lives reflect Christ in ways that manifest itself in community service and care. Instead, we try to manipulate our congregations into serving and attempt to make it as convenient as possible for them to serve others.

What about sacrifice? Christ makes it very clear that following him and serving others in his name will not be an easy task:

15. Dawn, A Royal "Waste" of Time, 124.
16. Tozer, Whatever Happened To Worship?, 18.
17. Dawn, A Royal "Waste" Of Time, 127.
18. Witvliet, Worship Seeking Understanding, 144.

Then Jesus told his disciples, "If anyone would come after me, let him deny himself and take up his cross and follow me." (Matt 16:24)

The cross is not fun. It is a tool of torture and excruciating pain.

Behold, I am sending you out as sheep in the midst of wolves, so be wise as serpents and innocent as doves. (Matt 10:16)

Following Jesus and serving others in his name should cost something of us. It will not always be easy, convenient, or fun.

Christians often have the tendency of focusing attention on reaching out to the world for God that they neglect getting to know God deeply themselves. Robert Mulholland states, "They were so busy *being in the world for God* that they failed to *be in God for the world.*"[19] I have known families who claim that doing sports on Sunday mornings is a form of evangelism. This may be the case, but what about their time of corporately worshiping with the body of Christ? How is the family receiving spiritual nourishment and guidance? Moreover, this may be evangelism for the parents (although I would argue that for many, what they call evangelism is not really evangelism), but what about the kids who are on the field playing the game? When do they get their corporate worship time? You cannot homeschool Christianity. The family component is vitally important in the discipleship journey, but the Christian life is one of community that requires the body of Christ, in all of it's beauty, and sometimes ugliness, to fulfill God's desire to make us more into the likeness of His Son. You must have consistency in your spiritual life in order to build relationships with people at church and to grow as a disciple of Christ. This is especially true of children as they are developing into the human beings God intends them to be.

I understand that sometimes parents feel they have no choice. Maybe their kid is in a sport they love and Sunday mornings are the only opportunity for them to play at this particular level. Maybe there is a certain obligation to the team because it is a tournament situation and either all play or nobody plays. Regardless, there is a long-term effect to missing church. Our society is set up to undermine the discipleship of our children and missing the gathering with the body of Christ on a regular basis is exactly what society is pushing us toward. I have personally seen the effects that choosing something other than church has had on families; even when they chose the other for good, possibly even spiritual, reasons. There are always

19. Mulholland, *The Deeper Journey*, 47.

deep regrets. The good has been chosen over the great. I'm not saying that church attendance is the goal, but church is a primary way in which God has provided us an opportunity to grow spiritually.

There is a reason Chick–fil–A restaurants are closed on Sundays. Can you imagine the criticism they've endured for that decision?[20] How much money is that business losing by choosing to be closed on Sunday? And yet, Chick–fil–A's founder Truett Cathy, a devout Christian, saw the importance of the gathered body of Christ and established early on in his company's history that his employees would be given the opportunity to actually take a Sabbath and go to church to worship with others.

The writer of the book of Hebrews pleads with the church to not neglect the corporate worship gathering:

> And let us consider how to stir up one another to love and good works, not neglecting to meet together, as is the habit of some, but encouraging one another, and all the more as you see the day drawing near. (Heb 10:24–25)

Scripture is clear that the gathering of worship is vitally important to our spiritual development. We will take a closer look at the importance of the gathering when we get to the chapter on corporate worship (chapter 8).

As we learn to worship better, every other aspect of our lives will become better. You see, corporate worship fuels evangelism. Service, including evangelism, is the natural byproduct of worship. As we worship, we are being drawn to the very being of God by reflecting the nature and being of his Son, Jesus. Jesus cared for the least of these and proclaimed the gospel. Our worship, therefore, leads us to care for the least of these and proclaim the gospel. We will discuss this further in the lifestyle worship chapter.

---

20. I have to admit, there have been times when I have been annoyed because what I craved for lunch after church was Chick–fil–A and my wife had to remind me that it was Sunday and they were closed. Noooo!

5

Who Is Welcome to Worship?

May all be welcomed here,
friend and stranger, from near and far.
May each be blessed and honoured
as they enter.
There is a friend's love
in the gentle heart of the Saviour.
For love of Him we offer friendship
and welcome every guest.

"CELTIC DAILY PRAYER"
PRAYERS AND READINGS
FROM THE NORTHUMBRIA COMMUNITY

THE PAGES OF SCRIPTURE show us that God invites all people to worship him. In fact, God's original plan in the Garden of Eden was for all of his creation to worship him in ways that honored and pleased him. Sure, the forms and guidelines for worship have changed over the years; Old Testament followers of God worshiped by means of animal sacrifice while the followers of Christ from the New Testament on, have gained direct access to God through Jesus Christ; but God's desire for his people to worship him has never changed nor diminished.

Who Did Jesus Welcome to Worship?

As we consider Jesus' life and ministry, we see that Jesus welcomed a variety of people from a variety of backgrounds:

Jesus Welcomed People of All Ages

The first chapter of John is just one example of many where adults are encouraged to worship Jesus. Here, Peter and Andrew are invited by Jesus to follow him and enter into discipleship with Jesus. The gospel writers also show that Jesus welcomed children into his presence (see Mark 9) while Matthew offers an example of a multitude of people, including adults and children, shouting praises as Jesus entered the city (see Matt 21). People of all ages have always been encouraged to worship God.

Jesus Welcomed People of All Ethnicities

In arguably the most popular worship passage in Scripture, John 4, Jesus offered the opportunity of worship to all people. His worship invitation to the Samaritan woman provided a preview of what his disciples would be commissioned to following his resurrection.

After his resurrection, Jesus commissioned his disciples to go to all the nations (Matt 28:19) and before his ascension back to heaven, Jesus told his disciples that the Holy Spirit will come upon them and they would receive power to be his witnesses "to the end of the earth" (Acts 1:8). And if there was any room for doubt, Paul was sent to the Jews to spread the gospel and Peter to the Greek and other non-Jewish people groups. People of all ethnicities are welcome to worship God—Father, Son, and Holy Spirit.

Jesus Welcomed People of All Social Status

Whether it was a fisherman or a tax collector, a religious leader or a poor widow, Jesus welcomed all people with open arms. The first chapter of Mark shows working class fishermen Peter, Andrew, James and John being called to Jesus' side at the Sea of Galilee while in Luke 19, Jesus shares the gospel with Zacchaeus, a well-known, and well-to-do, tax collector.

It didn't matter to Jesus what your social status was, you were welcome to worship in his presence.

Jesus Welcomed People of Questionable Nature

Jesus welcomed people with whom others would not associate. Jesus was called a "friend of sinners" (Matt 11:19; Luke 7:34). One such example is when Jesus allowed a prostitute to approach him at a dinner, in front of the religious leaders no less, and touch him.

> One of the Pharisees asked him to eat with him, and he went into the Pharisee's house and reclined at the table. And behold, a woman of the city, who was a sinner, when she learned that he was reclining at table in the Pharisee's house, brought an alabaster flask of ointment, and standing behind him at his feet, weeping, she began to wet his feet with her tears and wiped them with the hair of her head and kissed his feet and anointed them with the ointment. (Luke 7:36–38)

What was this woman doing in the Pharisee's house? Greek scholar William Barclay, says, "It was the custom that when a Rabbi was at a meal in such a house, all kinds of people came in—they were quite free to do so—to listen to the pearls of wisdom which fell from his lips."[1] It was not out of the ordinary for non-invited guests to be present at certain events. So we see that it was not her presence that caused a problem, it was her social status:

> Now when the Pharisee who had invited him saw this, he said to himself, "If this man were a prophet, he would have known who and what sort of woman this is who is touching him, for she is a sinner." (Luke 7:39)

But Jesus welcomes all people to worship him. For it is in the presence of Jesus that we find redemption, healing, peace . . . all that is right.

> Then turning toward the woman he said to Simon, "Do you see this woman? I entered your house; you gave me no water for my feet, but she has wet my feet with her tears and wiped them with her hair. You gave me no kiss, but from the time I came in she has not ceased to kiss my feet. You did not anoint my head with oil, but she has anointed my feet with ointment. Therefore I tell you, her sins, which are many, are forgiven—for she loved much. But

1. Barclay, *The Gospel of Luke*, 112.

he who is forgiven little, loves little." And he said to her, "Your sins are forgiven." Then those who were at table with him began to say among themselves, "Who is this, who even forgives sins?" And he said to the woman, "Your faith has saved you; go in peace." (Luke 7:44-50)

Whom Do We Welcome to Worship?

Now that we have seen who Jesus welcomed to worship, we must turn the tables and ask the harder question: Do we welcome people of all ages, all ethnicities, all social status, and questionable nature? If we are to be honest with ourselves, we must ask if we place expectations upon others by expecting them to dress a certain way, speak a certain way, like a certain style of music, and worship in a certain way? Do we set up barriers that others, or even ourselves, cannot break through in order to worship effectively?

The Church is to be a place where God is worshiped for who he is and praised for what he has done. The Church is to be a place where, like so many during Jesus' lifetime, hurting souls can come, meet the Great Physician and have their broken lives, hurting souls and damaged spirits healed and lifted up before the throne.

God is primarily concerned with our spiritual condition, but he is also concerned with our physical well-being. During His ministry, Jesus had large crowds following Him, wanting to be near Him. Some were there because they believed that Jesus was who he said he was, the Son of God. Others were curious and needed further convincing. But many were there simply because they knew Jesus had the power to heal. God's Church should be filled to capacity each and every weekend. Why? Is it because of a certain style of worship music or because of a really good preacher? No! It's because we have access to the throne of God where hurting souls can come and be made whole by the only One who has the power to heal.

It's difficult to understand, but there is a unique connection between praise and suffering, affliction, and adversity. God uses hard times to perfect, strengthen, and cleanse us. One way to get a healthy perspective on suffering is to consider this passage in the Book of Hebrews:

Although He was a Son, He learned obedience from what He suffered and, once made perfect, He became the source of eternal salvation for all who obey Him. (Heb 5:8-9)

Whether you are struggling with disease, problems in your marriage, depression, drugs, broken family—whatever your struggle—God can save you and heal you. All he wants from you in return is praise. The Old Testament prophet understood this concept and responded in this way:

> Though the fig tree should not blossom, nor fruit be on the vines, the produce of the olive fail and the fields yield no food, the flock be cut off from the fold and there be no herd in the stalls, yet I will rejoice in the Lord; I will take joy in the God of my salvation. (Hab 3:17–18)

I know it's hard to praise in moments of darkness, but that's exactly what will help you through difficult times. Just as precious metal must go through the refiner's fire before becoming a priceless work of art, or the crushing of tens of thousands of flower petals must occur to yield but an ounce of perfume, the sacrifice of praise is precious and sweet smelling to our heavenly Father.

William Cowper (pronounced "Cooper") was an English poet and hymn writer. Over the course of his lifetime, Cowper suffered from major bouts of depression leading him to attempt suicide on more than one occasion. After spending time in a mental institution, Cowper moved to the country town of Olney where he met the local pastor, John Newton. Cowper and Newton became close friends. Newton recognized that his friend struggled with depression and thought that he should help Cowper by engaging him in his writing of poetry. Newton suggested they co-author a book of hymns. This resulted in the creation of the *Olney Hymns*, which included Newton's "Amazing Grace" and Cowper's "There Is A Fountain Filled With Blood."

Though Cowper struggled with depression his entire life, there were times when the light broke through the darkness—and we know that light shines brightest in the dark. It was during these times that Cowper wrote his poetry/hymns praising God in the midst of his struggles. A hymn that came out of one of these experiences was "Sometimes a Light Surprises." Be blessed by these words:

> Sometimes a light surprises the Christian while he sings;
> It is the Lord, who rises with healing in His wings:
> When comforts are declining, He grants the soul again
> A season of clear shining, to cheer it after rain.

In holy contemplation we sweetly then pursue
The theme of God's salvation, and find it ever new.
Set free from present sorrow, we cheerfully can say,
Let the unknown tomorrow bring with it what it may.

It can bring with it nothing but He will bear us through;
Who gives the lilies clothing will clothe His people, too;
Beneath the spreading heavens, no creature but is fed;
And He Who feeds the ravens will give His children bread.

Though vine nor fig tree neither their wonted fruit should bear,
Though all the field should wither, nor flocks nor herds be there;
Yet God the same abiding, His praise shall tune my voice,
For while in Him confiding, I cannot but rejoice.[2]

King David knew the power of praising through hard times. When David committed adultery with Bathsheba and then planned her husband's murder to cover his sin, God confronted him though the prophet Nathan. Nathan shared God's verdict with the king: "Your son is going to die" (2 Sam 12:14). David immediately went into fasting and prayer and prostrated himself before God. A week later David heard the servants whispering and he knew his son was dead. He then did something that his servants thought was odd: David got up, cleaned himself up, and went into the house of the Lord to worship (2 Sam 12:20).

When you are in times of deep struggle, the only thing you can do that has any substance or value at all, is to worship! God's desire is that we worship him in good times and in bad. It is also his desire that all come to worship regardless of the circumstances. If we, for any reason, are putting up barriers for others or even ourselves when it comes to worshipping Jesus, then we need to immediately change our actions and ask God for forgiveness.

This call to worship provides us with a beautiful example of who is welcome to worship:

Ladies and Gentlemen
Boys and Girls—Welcome!
Believers and Seekers
And Those who have nowhere else to turn—Welcome!
Beggars and Bankers
Prostitutes and Professors—Welcome!

2. "Sometimes A Light Surprises" William Cowper, Public Domain, 1779.

Red, Brown, Yellow, Black, White
All precious in His sight—Welcome!
Politicians and Electricians
Beauticians and Physicians—Welcome!
Republicans and Democrats
If you're Skinny; if you're Fat—Welcome!
Those of you who own a FAX
If you cheat on income tax—Welcome!
Those of you who look so good
shiny hubcap, polished hood;
Those of you who've had a crash:
Banged and battered, maimed and mashed—Welcome!
Pro-Life, Pro-Choice
Pro-fane, Pro-vocative—Welcome!
Decrepit, divorced
Hopeless and Helpless—Welcome!
Adulterers and Athletes and Alcoholics
Victors and Victims—Welcome!
Sinners and Saints
Those who Sing and those who Paint—Welcome!
Hippies and Homosexuals and Handymen
Heroine Addicts and Hypocrites—Welcome!
Welcome to the Throne of Grace
God wants all to seek His face
None are worthy in this place
Bathe in His Amazing Grace.[3]

3. Jim Altizer. "Welcome to Worship." http://roadmapsforworship.com/?page_id=768

6

How Should We Worship?

Blessed is the time of waiting, when we stay awake for the Lord, the Creator of the universe, who fills all things and transcends all things. How I wish he would awaken me, his humble servant, from the sleep of slothfulness, even though I am of little worth. How I wish he would enkindle me with that fire of divine love. The flames of his love burn beyond the stars; the longing for his overwhelming delights and the divine fire ever burns within me!

COLUMBANUS
IRISH MONK, 6TH CENTURY

WORSHIP LEADER, AUTHOR AND teacher Tom Kraeuter states, "Worship is wholehearted, passionate adoration of our Creator/Redeemer."[1] In my own studies on worship, I have come to the conclusion that worship is predominately an action. Worship calls for participation. As we saw earlier, the most common Hebrew word for worship means "to bow down" and the most common Greek word for worship means "to kiss (the hand) toward." Worship in the true scriptural sense is not passive. Of course, there are exceptions to every rule: Jacob leaned on his staff while worshiping the Lord (Gen 47:31), although we must consider that Jacob was very old at this point and this was probably the best he could do to bow before God.

1. Kraeuter, *Worship Is...What?*, 25.

When looking at Scripture as a whole, we see that worship requires action from the worshiper.

> ... all Judah and the inhabitants of Jerusalem fell down before the Lord, worshiping the Lord. (2 Chr 20:18)

> And they bowed their heads and worshiped the Lord with their faces to the ground. (Neh 8:6)

> Oh come, let us worship and bow down; let us kneel before the Lord, our Maker. (Ps 95:6)

> And they came up and took hold of his feet and worshiped him. (Matt 28:9)

> ... present your bodies as a living sacrifice, holy and acceptable to God—which is your spiritual worship. (Rom 12:1)

> ... and so, falling on his face, he will worship God, and exclaim that God is really among you. (1 Cor 14:25)

> The twenty-four elders fall down before Him who is seated on the throne and worship him ... (Rev 4:10)

Worship must originate from the heart, but it cannot stay in the heart. Worship that is only heart is passive while worship that is only action is rote and empty ritual.[2] God desires worship that is heart and action.

Beyond the encouragement for worship to be participatory, we find little scriptural instruction for worship throughout the New Testament. Some have said this is because early Christians were Jewish and already knew how to worship. After all, they had generations of examples of worshipers who followed detailed instructions of worship provided by God for his people. They would have brought with them the traditions and liturgical practices of the Temple and the synagogue. There are others who use the analogy of Christianity as a relationship rather than a religion, and, therefore, harder to dictate exact requirements. Yet others struggle with the idea of guidelines for worship because we live in a culture that emphasizes fluid responsibility.

---

2. Note that I said "empty ritual." I believe rituals can be very good for us. I brush my teeth three times a day. This is a ritual in my life that is beneficial (not only for me but for others I come in contact with). Rituals such as reading the Bible every day, praying regularly, and gathering with the Body of Christ on Sunday mornings can be very beneficial for our spiritual growth. But "empty ritual," just going through the motions without heart, is meaningless. We must have a balance of heart and action as we worship the Lord.

There are, however, three general types of worship that I believe every Christian should practice: personal, corporate and lifestyle worship. I will unpack each of these in the next chapters.

PART TWO
Practices of Worship

The sun, moon, and stars, and the earth and waters, and all the trees of the field, and grass and herbs, and fishes and insects do glorify God. But herein is the peculiar dignity of the nature of man, that man is capable of glorifying God as Creator, and we do so with understanding, voluntarily, which is a heavenly work.

JONATHAN EDWARDS

THERE ARE THREE DIFFERENT types of worship that every Christian should practice. Each type is founded on biblical principles and is important to the development of the worshiper. As a way of responding to God's revelations, worshipers should practice personal, corporate and lifestyle worship.

7

Personal Worship

Only to sit and think of God,
Oh what a joy it is!
To think the thought, to breathe the Name;
Earth has no higher bliss.

FREDERICK W. FABER

THE FIRST TYPE OF worship every Christian should practice is personal worship. Christ followers should develop consistent habits of dedicated times of personal worship. This is important in the development of one's relationship with the Lord. In fact, it is the primary way in which we develop a relationship with God.

Personal worship is a time for us to tune our ears, and our hearts, to hear God's voice. There is a connection between God and his people as the Extraordinary dwells with the ordinary. We must be careful not to think that we initiate this connection, for it is God who has graciously and lovingly revealed himself to us. God is the initiator of worship causing us to respond in awe—echoing the words of Isaiah "Woe to me! I am ruined" (see Isa 6:5; NIV).

The practice of personal worship has been described in many ways. Oswald Chambers, in his devotional *My Utmost for His Highest*, called it "communion with God." A.W. Tozer described it as "the continuous and unembarrassed interchange of love and thought between God and the soul of redeemed man."[1] Dallas Willard called it the "renovation of the heart."

Practically speaking, what is personal worship? Personal worship is that time you set aside to be in God's presence . . . alone. You do not have to be alone, but you are not intentionally worshiping with others. Personal worship includes praying to, meditating on, thinking about, singing to and listening for God. It is reading your Bible on the front porch swing. It is grabbing your guitar and singing praises to God in the privacy of your bedroom. It is meditating, which means to pray, think and listen, on God in the backyard garden. It's all of these and more.

The Apostle Paul makes it clear that as we participate in personal worship, we are developing an intimate relationship with God:

> That you, being rooted and established in love, may have power, together with all the saints, to grasp how wide and long and high and deep is the love of Christ, and to know this love that surpasses knowledge—that you may be filled to the measure of all the fullness of God. (Eph 3:17–19)

Our personal worship plants our hearts deep in the love of God so that we might know how wide, long, high and deep his love for us truly is. This is the love in which we are meant to dwell. God's love for us, shown through the sending of his Son, provides a way for us to dwell with him. When we realize just how abundant God's love for us is, how can we not respond in worship and praise? One of my favorite hymns expresses just how great God's love for us truly is:

> The love of God is greater far
> Than tongue or pen can ever tell.
> It goes beyond the highest star
> And reaches to the lowest hell.
> The guilty pair, bowed down with care,
> God gave His Son to win;
> His erring child He reconciled
> And pardoned from his sin.
>
> Could we with ink the ocean fill,
> And were the skies of parchment made;
> Were every stalk on earth a quill,
> And every man a scribe by trade;
> To write the love of God above

1. Tozer, *The Pursuit of God*, 15.

Would drain the ocean dry;
Nor could the scroll contain the whole,
Though stretched from sky to sky.

O love of God, how rich and pure!
How measureless and strong!
It shall forevermore endure
The saints' and angels' song.[2]

Again, I have to ask: When we realize just how abundant, measureless and strong God's love for us is, how can we not respond in worship and praise?

Have you ever had a time in your life when you just needed to get away, find a quiet place and simply focus on God; a time to forget about the worries of your day, and life, and concentrate on your Maker? I think we all go through times like that. Maybe you're going through one of those times right now. As a follower of Christ, it is important for us to spend one-on-one time with God on a regular basis. There are many ways we can do this: devotions or "quiet times"; prayer; journaling; singing; meditation (thinking upon); reading the Bible. All of these, and more, when done between you and God, is what is called personal worship.

For some of us, these are great things that we'd love to have time to do. But sometimes there are just not enough hours in the day to get everything done. So instead of "making the time" to do these, we conclude that the Sunday morning worship services are our times of worship. But what about your personal worship? You see, Sunday morning worship services are great worship times, but that is corporate worship. When someone else joins me in worship it is no longer personal worship. It has turned into corporate worship. (The question as to whether personal worship occurs during corporate gatherings is another discussion all together. One we will look at in the next chapter). If we wait until Sunday morning to worship God we miss a large part of worship—our personal connection with God.

We all worship, all the time. You may think you are waiting until Sunday to worship, but in fact you are worshiping all throughout the week. The question is, who—or better yet—what are you worshiping? Harold Best states,

> ...nobody does not worship...at this very moment, and for as long as this world endures, everybody inhabiting it is bowing down and serving something or someone—an artifact, a person, an institution,

2. "The Love of God" Frederick M. Lehman, Public Domain, 1919.

an idea, a spirit, or God through Christ . . . we are, every one of us, unceasing worshipers and will remain so forever . . .[3]

A true worshiper is one who daily seeks the Lord in private, acknowledging him through the mundane activities of life, while maintaining a kingdom perspective and attitude. As Marva Dawn rightfully acknowledges with the title of her book "A Royal 'Waste' of Time," we must "waste" our time on God by daily expending an excessive amount of energy and resources on offering God the worship that he is due. If I am unable to offer myself to God on a daily basis during the week, do I really have any business going to church on Sunday to rehearse the truths of the faith that I clearly can't live by the other six days of the week?

When we come together on Sundays for worship, our corporate worship should be fueled by the personal worship in which we have participated throughout the week. Then, as we gather, our corporate worship can help fuel our personal worship for the week to come. We must worship God through personal acts of worship throughout the week until we meet again to worship Him through corporate acts of worship on Sunday. Let's not be too busy during the week to meet with the One who has given everything for us.

3. Best, *Unceasing Worship*, 17.

8

Corporate Worship

Therefore, let him who until now has had the privilege of living in common Christian life with other Christians praise God's grace from the bottom of his heart. Let him thank God on his knees and declare: It is grace, nothing but grace, that we are allowed to live in community with Christian brethren.

DIETRICH BONHOEFFER

GOD CALLS THE CORPORATE gathering of worshipers the body of Christ. It should be no surprise then to hear that the English word corporate is derived from the Latin word *corpus*, meaning the human body. Some question whether or not the corporate gathering is necessary believing that personal worship is enough for developing their relationship with God. C.S. Lewis counters,

> I thought that I could do it on my own, by retiring to my rooms and reading theology, and I wouldn't go to the churches . . . But as I went on I saw the great merit of it. I came up against different people of quite different outlooks and different education, and then gradually my conceit just began peeling off. I realized that the hymns (which were just sixth-rate music) were, nevertheless, being sung with devotion and benefit by an old saint in elastic-side boots in the opposite pew, and then you realize that you aren't fit to clean those boots. It gets you out of your solitary conceit.[1]

1. Lewis, *God In the Dock*, 61–62.

In addition to personal worship, Christians should practice corporate worship. Martin Luther states, that, "to gather with God's people in united adoration of the Father is as necessary to the Christian life as prayer." Worship is not only a personal experience, but also a group endeavor. The Apostle Peter speaks of Christ-followers in terms like "people," "priesthood," and "nation." Jesus said, "For where two or three come together in my name, there I am with them" (Matt 18:20). This is not to say that Christ manifests himself in ways to the gathering than He does to the individual, for we know that God does not change. We are the ones who change as "me" becomes "we."

In corporate worship, gathered Christians reflect the very nature of the triune God, simultaneously singular and plural, and experience God corporately through both the presence of the Holy Spirit, and through one another. There is also a dual audience in corporate worship, reflected in Paul's writings to the Ephesians: "Speak to one another with psalms, hymns and spiritual songs. Sing and make music in your heart to the Lord, always giving thanks to God the Father for everything, in the name of our Lord Jesus Christ" (Eph 5:19-20). We sing to God and to one another.

I can't tell you how many times I have been led into worship by observing someone else worshiping. There is encouragement found in seeing others worship God with all they have and all they are.

A number of years ago I was sitting with a friend as he told me his wife was just diagnosed with cancer. I couldn't believe it. I didn't want to believe it. She was young and full of energy (more energy than I could ever muster). They had three young children that were good friends with my kids. Our families had built a close relationship over the years. When he told me this devastating news, many questions swirled around in my mind: How could this be happening? What purpose could there be? Why would God allow this?

My friend told me on a Wednesday. They decided to hold off on telling the church family until they could personally tell those that needed to hear it directly from them. As a result, not many people knew of the diagnosis as we gathered for worship on Sunday. I remember that day clearly because it opened my eyes to a greater understanding of corporate worship.

I was serving as the Worship Pastor at the church and happened to have that particular Sunday off the platform as one of my worship leaders was scheduled to lead. My wife and I were sitting near the back of the sanctuary, which we rarely ever do (we usually sit near the front). At one moment during the musical worship portion of the service I had a strong sense to turn my eyes toward the opposite side of the sanctuary. As I did, I saw my good friend, who had just been diagnosed with cancer a few days earlier, with eyes raised and hands lifted, singing:

In You, in You I find my peace
In You, in You I find my strength
In You, I live and move and breathe
Let everything I say and do be founded by my faith in You
I lift up holy hands and sing, let the praises ring.[2]

My breath was taken away and I started to cry. She entered into worship with complete abandon, in the midst of struggle, pain and uncertainty, and it encouraged my heart to worship. Although she didn't know it, she helped to usher me into worship. I would have missed that beautiful example of worship, had I not participated in corporate worship.

Too often worshipers engage in personal worship in a corporate setting. I believe this to be a big area that the church struggles with today, especially in North America. We live in a narcissistic culture where it is expected, and even encouraged, to do anything, at all costs, to get ahead. It doesn't matter who you have to step on to get where you are going, just do what helps you. I see this every day on the streets of Southern California as drivers cut off other commuters and have no regard for their fellow travelers. This narcissistic attitude has made its way in to the church where worship has become primarily about what I want and what I feel I need, or deserve. As a result, worship leaders have made an effort to reverse the affects of narcissism by encouraging people to focus on God whatever the cost. And a big part of that cost has been corporate worship. We enter the sanctuary and as soon as the music begins, we close our eyes, lift our hands, and ignore everyone else around us. I've even heard leaders encourage the congregation to do so—"Don't worry about what anyone else is doing, just do what helps you worship." But that is not corporate worship.

The Apostle Paul encourages the church to not only worship in a vertical manner—with our attention and focus on God—but to also worship horizontally, encouraging one another in our worship. Paul thought this was so important that he mentions it in two different letters:

... be filled with the Spirit, *addressing one another* in psalms and hymns and spiritual songs, singing and making melody to the Lord

2. "Let the Praises Ring" Lincoln Brewster ©2002 Integrity's Praise! Music.

with your heart, giving thanks always and for everything to God the Father in the name of our Lord Jesus Christ. (Eph 5:18b–20, *emphasis* mine)

Let the word of Christ dwell in you richly, *teaching and admonishing one another* in all wisdom, singing psalms and hymns and spiritual songs, with thankfulness in your hearts to God. (Col 3:16, *emphasis* mine)

We live in a time when corporate worship is misunderstood. What people think is corporate worship is actually personal worship happening in a corporate setting. There are 168 hours in a week. For 167 of those hours we get to practice personal worship. We essentially only have one hour a week to engage in corporate worship with the Body of Christ. We must be zealous for that hour and protect it at all costs. Let's not waste that time away by worshiping personally during a time set aside for corporate worship. When we do, we may miss an opportunity to be led into worship by those around us, or worst yet, we may miss the opportunity to be an encouragement to someone else in their worship.

I'd like to speak for a moment to worship leaders and those that plan corporate worship. It is important to plan our worship services in ways that encourage corporate worship rather than personal worship in a corporate setting. Do the songs, prayers, Scripture readings, etc. that you have planned for the service encourage corporate worship? Does the way you have set up the worship space encourage personal or corporate worship?[3]

A few years ago, while on vacation with my family, we visited a friend's church. This is a large church with multiple services. I have been to this church a few times and appreciate their leadership and ministries. On this particular weekend, we attended the Saturday evening service. I would guess there were probably five hundred people in attendance at this service. Just before the sermon, the worship leader led the congregation in a song that, in one fell swoop, forced me, and the entire congregation, into personal worship. At one point in the song, the lyrics state, "It's just you and me here Jesus; Only you and me here now." I had to stop singing when we reached this point in the song. The lyrics did not match the reality of the

---

3. Side note: Turning the house lights off during corporate worship generally encourages personal worship and has the potential to enhance a performance mentality among both the worship leaders and the congregation. After all, if it looks and sounds like a concert they would attend on Friday night, why would we expect the congregation to feel any differently on a Sunday morning?

situation. It was not only 'Jesus and me' present at that moment. My wife was standing next to me, as were our two friends. Not to mention the other four hundred and ninety-six other people in the sanctuary. If I were to sing those words, 1) I would have been a liar, and 2) it would have forced me to ignore everyone else in that room.

I know you may be thinking, "Oh, you're being too literal!" But if Jesus claimed to be Truth (see John 14:6), and we gather in his name to worship him, isn't it important for us to be truthful as we worship? Shouldn't we be concerned with whether or not the words we sing in worship are truthful? A. W. Tozer has been quoted as saying, "Christians don't tell lies they just go to church and sing them." Oh, if that were only hyperbole. Too often, the words we sing in worship do not find their way to the reality of our lives. There are so many things in this world that are vying for our attention and trying to pull us away from God. When I gather for worship, I want to declare worship for who God is and praise for what he has done. And I want to be truthful as I sing the songs. Anything less is a waste of time for God and for the worshiper.

In consideration of corporate worship, Orthodox theologian Alexander Schmemann states,

> The journey begins when Christians leave their homes and beds. They leave, indeed, their life in this present and concrete world, and whether they have to drive fifteen miles or walk a few blocks, a sacramental act is already taking place, an act which is the very condition of everything else that is to happen. For they are now on their way to constitute the Church, or to be more exact, to be transformed into the Church of God. They have been individuals, some white, some black, some poor, some rich, they have been the "natural" world and a natural community. And now they have been called to "come together in one place," to bring their lives, their very "world" with them and to be more than what they were: a new community with a new life. We are already far beyond the categories of common worship and prayer. The purpose of this "coming together" is not simply to add a religious dimension to the natural community, to make it "better"—more responsible, more Christian. The purpose is to fulfill the Church, and that means to make present the One in whom all things are at their end, and all things are at their beginning. [4]

4. Schmemann, *For the Life of the World*, 26–27. Used by permission.

As mentioned in an earlier chapter, we must not neglect the power and importance of the corporate worship experience. Think of the corporate gathering as a bonfire with each piece of wood symbolizing a Christ–follower. When together, the flame burns brightly and with intensity. But take one of those logs out of the fire and put it off by itself and the flame quickly diminishes. Now, take that same piece of wood and put it back into the fire and it reignites and burns brightly with the other pieces of wood. Puritan Stephen Charnock considered the power of corporate worship:

> Public worship keeps up the memorials of God in a world prone to atheism, and a sense of God in a heart prone to forgetfulness. The angels sung in company, not singly, at the birth of Christ, and praised God not only with a simple elevation of their spiritual nature, but audibly, by forming a voice in the air. Affections are more lively, spirits more raised in public than private . . . fire increaseth by laying together many coals on one place; so is devotion inflamed by the union of many hearts, and by a joint presence.[5]

Once we understand the importance of corporate worship, we must consider those things that are indispensable to a corporate worship gathering. Many theologians consider these six elements that emerge from the New Testament as essential for corporate worship:

1. Reading the Word (1 Tim 4:13–15)

2. Preaching (Acts 2:42; 1 Tim 4:13; 2 Tim 3:15–17; 4:2)

3. Praying (1 Tim 2:1; 1 Cor 14:16; Heb 4:16; cf. Acts 1:14; 2:1; 4:24, 32)

4. Singing (Eph 5:19; Col 3:16; Rev 5:9–13; 15:3, 4)

5. Regularly observing baptism (Matt 28:19, 20; cf. Acts 2:41; 8:12, 36–38; 9:18) and the Lord's Supper (Acts 2:42; 1 Cor 11:24–30)

6. Regularly giving to the work of the Word (1 Cor 16:2; 2 Cor 9:7)

Other worship practices are helpful but definitely not necessary. For instance, we use instruments to accompany our congregational singing and offer musical praise to God, but the New Testament is silent when it comes to instructions on the use of instruments in worship. When we seek authentic connection with God in worship, we should expect to find him within the above essential elements. In his perfect wisdom, God has given us these clear principles and practices to guide our corporate worship.

5. Charnock, *Discourses upon the Existence and Attributes of God*, 221.

Worshiping together is critically important to our being Christ-followers. When we gather to worship, we don't merely gather with friends to sing and pray together. As the people of God, we have the privilege of entering into the very presence of God. Encountering God in corporate worship is the very nature of the church. To be the church is to gather in God's presence and worship him together.

9

Lifestyle Worship

The knowledge of God is born out of obedience.

JOHN CALVIN

In addition to personal and corporate worship, the disciple of Christ should engage in a lifestyle of worship. Practicing lifestyle worship means that Christ–followers demonstrate their love, and thereby their worship, through their obedience to God. As one of the premier thinkers on worship, Robert Webber was once asked, "How do I know if I have truly worshiped?" Webber's response was simple, "To the extent that you have obeyed." Jesus said, "Whoever has my commands and obeys them, he is the one who loves me" (John 14:21). In his classic work *Celebration of Discipline*, Richard Foster states, "Just as worship begins in holy expectancy, it ends in holy obedience. If worship does not propel us into greater obedience, it has not been worship."[1] It is through our obedience to God that we truly live a life of worship.

The Apostle Paul's teaching on worship urged Christians to consider the mercies they had received, and to worship by offering themselves as a living sacrifice (Rom 12:1). We're not talking about living a perfect life, as Scripture never demands perfection. The life of a worshiper is fueled by God's mercies compelling us to live a life that is pleasing to God—a life of obedience. The prophet Micah gives us a wonderful description of lifestyle worship:

1. Foster, *Celebration of Discipline*, 148.

> He has told you, O man, what is good; and what does the Lord
> require of you but to do justice, and to love kindness, and to walk
> humbly with your God? (Mic 6:8)

When you act justly, caring for those in need; love and share kindness with others; and keep in step with God the Father, Son, and Holy Spirit; you live a life of worship.

When the disciples were called to follow Jesus, their lives were radically changed. Spending time with Jesus and following him meant discovering the world through the eyes of God. The compassion of God is clearly seen to include the poor and needy, the sick and dying—physically, emotionally, mentally and spiritually. If we are to worship Jesus, then we are to live our lives as Jesus lived:

> Then Jesus told his disciples, "If anyone would come after me, let
> him deny himself and take up his cross and follow me. For who-
> ever would save his life will lose it, but whoever loses his life for my
> sake will find it." (Matt 16:24–25)

This call to follow Jesus enlarges our vision for what it means to live with God, and consequently, worship him. In fact, Jesus says that our worship of him will be measured by how we live (see Matt 25:31–46).

God expects faithful worshipers to live in such a way that their lives demonstrate righteousness and justice. The world is meant to see and know something about God by the way faithful worshipers live out their lives. Mark Labberton suggests,

> The crisis the church currently faces is that our individual and cor-
> porate worship do not produce the fruit of justice and righteous-
> ness that God seeks. This creates a crisis of faithfulness before God
> and a crisis of purpose before the world. Scripture indicates that
> our personal and communal worship are meant to shape our vision
> and fire our engines to be daring disciples, imitating and sharing
> the love of Jesus Christ in acts of righteousness and justice. What's
> more, the Bible teaches that the people of the world, whether they
> believe it or not, suffer and die while waiting for us in the church
> to live like the people of God, demonstrating our worship with our
> lives (Rom 8:18–25). The heart of the battle over worship is this:
> our worship practices are separated from our call to justice and,
> worse, foster the self-indulgent tendencies of our culture rather
> than nurturing the self-sacrificing life of the kingdom of God. We

are asleep. Nothing is more important than for us to wake up and practice the dangerous act of worship, living God's call to justice.[2]

Living a lifestyle of worship means dwelling where the heart of God is and showing our worship in lives that embody his loving righteousness and merciful justice.

> Our worship should lead us to greater mercy. Our worship should lead us to costly acts of justice, especially for those who are the least seen, the least remembered, the least desired.
>
> Vigorous biblical practice of worship should stop, or at least redirect, our endless consumerism, as our free choice to spend less in order to give away more. Our worship should be recognizable by the lives it produces, ones that plainly evidence the broad, sacrificial and persevering commitment of Jesus Christ. Our community reputation, as Scripture suggests, should be that the church comprises those who pursue justice for the poor and oppressed because that is what it means to be Christ's body in the world. We should not fool ourselves into thinking that it's enough to feel drawn to the heart of God without our lives showing the heart of God.[3]

Worshipers must demonstrate their worship by doing justice, loving kindness, and walking humbly with the triune God.

This is not to say that Christians have a free pass from sharing the gospel of Jesus Christ through words. The declaration of Christ's love through spoken words is invaluable and must not be denied, yet our lives must also declare the truth of God in ways that publish the good news of Jesus Christ. Thirteenth century preacher Francis of Assisi is quoted as saying, "Preach the gospel at all times and when necessary use words." Although Francis was a powerful preacher, he also understood the power of lifestyle worship.

Throughout the past few chapters we have looked at three types of worship every Christian should practice. No one type is more important than another. Each is invaluable and each is biblical. Worshipers must practice personal, corporate and lifestyle worship. Now, let's take a look at the different types of gatherings in which worshipers participate.

2. Labberton, *The Dangerous Act of Worship*, 22–23.
3. Ibid., 38.

PART THREE
Gatherings of Worship

Whenever His people gather and worship Him, God promises He will make His presence known in their midst. On the other hand, where God's people consistently neglect true spiritual worship, His manifest presence is rarely experienced.

RALPH MAHONEY

IF YOU ARE A ministry leader in a church, you have probably heard the following question more than a few times: "Why can't worship at our church be more like the worship at [fill in the blank]?" Students come back from a mountaintop experience at summer camp and long to have the same type of worship experience at church. Men return from Promise Keeper's and wonder why the singing at church never sounds the same as at the event. Worship team members attend a worship conference and come back to church deflated because the worship service at church doesn't have the same level of quality or energy.

A few years ago I read two writings that helped put words to what my heart has always known—there is a difference in the gatherings, which explains the divergence of worship experiences. I am grateful to Paul B. Clark Jr.[4] and Syd Hielema[5] for the worship gathering titles in the next chapters.

4. Clark, *Tune My Heart To Sing Thy Grace*, 2010.
5. Syd Hielema. "The Festival–Envy Syndrome: Four Contexts of Worship." *Reformed Worship*, March 2004.

There are four types of worship gatherings in which a Christian can participate. These gatherings include Private Worship, Family Worship, Congregational Worship and Festival Worship.

10

The Private Worship Gathering

Be still, and know that I am God.

PSALM 46:10

PRIVATE WORSHIP IS A time of worshiping in isolation. It is in this gathering where the personal worship elements from chapter seven are put into practice. Though it may seem strange to think of in the terms of a gathering, it is accurate to consider the Private Worship Gathering as an assembly of the worshiper and the triune God—Father, Son, and Holy Spirit. Paul B. Clark Jr. states, "The solitude of worship which seems exclusive in that only the single worshiper gathers with the triune God may find many means of expression, and a variety of places for the gathering itself."[1] As I gather with the triune God during my daily devotional time, I am provided with an opportunity to realize who God is and how he has revealed himself to me. Private worship is not exclusive to a specific place. It may occur in my backyard as I read my Bible, at the kitchen table as I drink my morning cup of coffee, or any other number of places. It is the time I set aside to focus on God and offer him glory.

Private worship does not only happen during designated times, but may also occur during unplanned times. For instance, if I find myself stuck in traffic on the highway (I live in Los Angeles so this is a rather common occurrence) I am provided the opportunity to plug in my iPod and sing songs in

1. Clark, *Tune My Heart*, 42.

praise to the Lord. If I find myself waiting longer for a meeting to begin than expected, I can use that time to connect with God through prayer.

The Private Worship Gathering is often intimate and personal. The songs that are sung and the prayers that are prayed in this gathering may be too intimate for a public worship setting. We find many examples of this as King David cried out to the Lord from the depths of his soul:

> How long, O Lord? Will you forget me forever? How long will you hide your face from me? How long must I take counsel in my soul and have sorrow in my heart all the day? How long shall my enemy be exalted over me? (Ps 13:1–2)

Or,

> My God, my God, why have you forsaken me? Why are you so far from saving me, from the words of my groaning? O my God, I cry by day, but you do not answer, and by night, but I find no rest. (Ps 22:1–2)

And yet, even through times of deep crying out to the Lord, we can rejoice in God's faithfulness, knowing he will hold us in his mighty hand:

> But I have trusted in your steadfast love; my heart shall rejoice in your salvation. I will sing to the Lord, because he has dealt bountifully with me. (Ps 13:5–6)

Oftentimes, certain intimate worship elements that would be better suited for the Private Worship Gathering are incorporated into corporate settings. Worship leaders must be careful of this and should reserve these intimate songs, prayers, etc. for private worship. "But this is the only opportunity for our congregation to worship with this particular song!" This is why we must encourage our people to engage in personal worship throughout the week (review chapter seven). We must teach our people to worship at all times, not just on Sunday mornings.

An important form of worship that is appropriate for the Private Worship Gathering but is often neglected in today's worship culture is silence.[2] Too often we feel as though the only way to respond to God is through the use of words. Yet it is in times of silence that we are able to listen to God's voice as he speaks to us. Clark states,

---

2. I believe silence is also heavily neglected in congregational worship gatherings. This is something worship leaders and pastors should consider incorporating more regularly.

Many Christians seem to have need of constant noise in searching for inspiration to move them toward a sense of nearness to God. While playing the music of Christian artists may drown out some of the world's distractions, if we are not careful, it may cover the "still small voice" of God himself. Worship communion in solitude would seem to be well served at times by the discipline of silence.[3]

Henri Nouwen shares that,

> When Arsenius, the Roman educator who exchanged his status and wealth for the solitude of the Egyptian desert, prayed, "Lord, lead me into the way of salvation," he heard a voice saying, "Be silent."[4]

It is silence that completes and intensifies the solitude found in the Private Worship Gathering. This is the conviction shared by the Desert Fathers. There is a story about Abbot Macarius that makes this point well.

> Once the abbot Macarius, after he had given the benediction to the brethren in the church at Scete, said to them, "Brethren, fly." One of the elders answered him, "How can we fly further than this, seeing we are here in the desert?" Then Macarius placed his finger on his mouth and said, "Fly from this." So saying, he entered his cell and shut the door.[5]

But how do we worship through silence when we are so out of practice? If you are anything like me, sitting for an extended period of time in silence, focusing solely on God, without your mind wandering, is a difficult task. Maybe you can agree with the great English poet John Donne who said,

> I throw myself down in my chamber, and I call in and invite God and his angels thither; and when they are there, I neglect God and his angels for the noise of a fly, for the rattling of a coach, or the whining of a door.[6]

Worshiping through silence is a spiritual discipline, and just like any discipline, it takes concentrated effort (practice) to do well. It is called a discipline for a reason. We must be disciplined if we are to worship God through silence amidst an overly talkative world.

3. Clark, *Tune My Heart*, 42-43.

4. Nouwen, *The Way of the Heart*, 35.

5. Hannay, *The Wisdom of the Desert*, 111.

6. Donne, *LXXX Sermons* (1640) 12 December 1626 'At the Funeral of Sir William Cokayne'.

For those who struggle with incorporating silence in worship, one way you can begin to practice silence is through the exercise of *Lectio Divina*.[7] *Lectio Divina*, or "Divine Reading," can be described as "the deepening of an interpersonal relationship."[8] It provides a spiritual rhythm for offering yourself to God and embracing all God has to offer. *Lectio Divina* is a slow, contemplative praying through the Scriptures and begins by cultivating the ability to listen deeply. The voice of the Lord often speaks very softly. In order to hear someone speaking softly, you must be silent. Once you have gotten yourself in the habit of meditating on the Word of God through an exercise such as *Lectio Divina*, you can then begin to incorporate dedicated times of silence into your private worship of God.

Many people do not personally prepare before a worship service and furthermore struggle to clear their minds to focus on God in worship. Private Worship allows us to focus and prepare to worship with other believers. The practice of spiritual disciplines during Private Worship will assist in our practice of worship during Congregational Gatherings. Ultimately, the primary purpose of the Private Worship Gathering is to worship God in intimate ways that encourage personal devotion and discipleship.

7. *Lectio Divina* may be done in private or as a group exercise. See Appendix 4 for instruction on how to practice *Lectio Divina*.

8. Hall, *Too Deep For Words*, 26.

11

The Family Worship Gathering

*The most important and highest activity that a company of God's people could
ever engage in, is to offer Almighty God acceptable worship.*

DAVID MARTIN LLOYD–JONES

WHEN WE TALK ABOUT the Family Worship Gathering, we do not simply
mean that those gathered together are related by blood or genealogy. This
worship gathering considers the familial or familiar components of the word
and not just the immediate family unit. An eighteenth century definition of
"family" includes "any group of things classed as kindred based on common
distinguishing characteristics." Hence, Family Worship occurs when small
group gatherings, made up of people who are familiar to one another, worship
together.

When this type of group gathers, they may not have met with the intention
of worshiping together, but some form of worship ends up occurring. For example, the elders of the church hold their monthly elder meeting and at the close of
the meeting they spend an extended time in prayer. They have gathered for the
purpose of having a business meeting, but conclude the meeting by participating
in worship. A group of friends gather at someone's house for dinner and end up
standing around the piano singing favorite hymns. They have gathered for the
purpose of fellowship, but wind down the evening with worship.

The Family Worship environment is distinguished by its ability to deepen
interpersonal relationships.

Most churches are made up of small groups inside the larger congregation. In addition to the nuclear families, congregations encourage gatherings of senior adults, newlywed couples, young parents, and singles. Many who attend church find important and meaningful relationship through such groupings.[1]

At a church where I served as Worship Pastor, I was part of a weekly small group that met together for dinner, fellowship and prayer. The evening would begin with families gathered in the backyard as the children played. This was always a particularly enjoyable time as we would catch up on the week's activities. Once everyone arrived we would share a meal together. At the conclusion of dinner, we would gather in the living room to pray, laugh and sometimes cry together. Many of us are still very close to this day, although most have moved on from that church. A strong bond was forged because we engaged in Family Worship.

The deep interpersonal relationships developed in the Family Worship Gathering are invaluable to the body of Christ. This gathering provides an opportunity for the church to build relationships with one another in ways that no other worship gathering offers. Within the Family Worship Gathering friendships develop into real and transparent relationships. Friends become family as the group lives out biblical love for one another. This worship gathering provides a perfect opportunity to put into practice the "one anothers" found throughout the New Testament: to love one another, be devoted to one another, accept one another, and serve one another (just to name a few). One of the more important "one anothers" that this worship gathering helps to fulfill is the opportunity to pray deeply for one another.

As the Worship Pastor at my church, it is my calling to spiritually lead and direct the members of the worship ministry, as well as the congregation. At the beginning of every worship team rehearsal, I gather the team together for a time of prayer. We share requests and take turns praying for one another. The team has begun to share deep personal requests as they have grown together spiritually. The worship team has become a family, willing to share even their deepest needs, struggles and desires. In a large group setting, it is easy to blend in and get lost, but not in a small group. No one is overlooked in the Family Worship gathering.

Ultimately, the primary purpose of the Family Worship gathering is to deepen interpersonal relationships within the group, encouraging one another toward Christ–likeness through accountability and discipleship.

1. Clark, *Tune My Heart*, 44.

12

The Congregational Worship Gathering

As long as you notice, and have to count the steps, you are not yet dancing but only learning to dance. A good shoe is a shoe you don't have to notice. Good reading becomes possible when you need not consciously think about eyes, or light, or print, or spelling. The perfect church service would be one we were almost unaware of; our attention would have been on God.

C.S. LEWIS

CONGREGATIONAL WORSHIP IS THE type of gathering that is most often considered when thinking about the gathering of worshipers. It is within this gathering that the corporate worship practices of chapter eight are accomplished. This is the week-in, week–out corporate worship experience. It is the regular routine of gathering with others in order to respond to all God has revealed of himself. It is very much like telling your spouse you love them every day. Sure, you told them yesterday, and they should remember, but anyone who has been in a relationship any length of time knows that the regular acknowledgement of one another maintains the relationship and encourages its health and vitality. The weekly gathering of the congregation for worship, deepens the bonds within the body of Christ—bonds strengthened through years of faithfulness, shared experiences, and, sometimes, even conflict. Hielema shares,

> Worshipers of all ages gather in a wide variety of focused and unfocused, expectant and unexpectant mindsets. On our left sits an old friend whom we love dearly, while behind us on the right we find the

young man with whom we argued so vehemently at last week's committee meeting.[1]

This is the beauty of congregational worship—it is offered by the body of Christ.

> The Apostle Paul described the body of Christ not in a homogeneous way, but as being composed of old and young (Titus 2:2–6); rich and poor (1 Cor 11:21–22); of varied giftedness (1 Cor 12:4); mixed in race, gender and status (Gal 3:28; 1 Cor 12:13). It is tempting to simplify things by narrowing or targeting the population of your Church, but Paul makes the case that homogeneity (sameness) actually cripples the body of Christ (1 Cor 12:19). Unity, on the other hand, verifies both the Truth and love of God. Unity within diversity is the way of Christ. Consequently, when outsiders see the proverbial ballerina, punked-out teenager, brain-surgeon and custodian all worshiping together, they are convinced of the real Jesus, and of his love for his people. They know something supernatural is going on."[2]

Jesus loves all people and desires for them to worship him in spirit and truth (John 4:24).

Worship Is About Style

I'm sure you've heard it said that worship is not about style. Although I understand the basic sentiment and the purpose behind the statement, I would have to disagree from a broader viewpoint. Worship is about style. If we are to offer multi-cultural worship to our multi-faceted God, then our worship must contain a variety of cultural styles, all working together to glorify God.

Every worshiper is different. As the church gathers to worship our great God, we find a collection of people of varying ages, ethnicities, and even cultures. Culture can be defined as the behaviors and beliefs characteristic of a particular social, ethnic, or age group. For our purposes, I will separate the terms multi-cultural and multi-ethnic. Culture may be linked to ethnicity, but ethnicity does not always mandate culture. For example, an African-American growing up in Texas may be raised to love country

1. Syd Hielema. "The Festival-Envy Syndrome: Four Contexts of Worship." *Reformed Worship*, March 2004, 4.

2. Altizer, *The Making Of A Worship Leader*, 52.

music and wear a cowboy hat and boots or a white Anglo–American growing up in Downtown Detroit may be raised to love the music of Motown,
rap and hip–hop. I will examine the term "culture" from an American an-
thropological viewpoint, looking at the distinct ways that people classify
and represent their experiences and actions, regardless of ethnicity.

Multi–Cultural Worship

Just as Jesus was born into a particular culture milieu, so every Christian
worships from a specific cultural perspective. As the church gathers for
worship, experiences and behaviors accompany the worshiper. There is an
old Latin saying, *lex orandi, lex credendi,* which roughly means, the way in
which we worship is the way in which we believe. Our worship is shaped by
our beliefs and experiences . . . and our beliefs are shaped by our worship.

When it comes to musical worship, culture plays a significant role in
our musical preferences. If we were raised on classical music, our worship
preference will lean toward classic worship. If we were raised listening to
contemporary pop, we will lean toward praise choruses. If we were raised in
a family that cherished the singing of traditional hymns, then we will want
those same hymns incorporated in our worship gatherings. Even if we are
not aware of our cultural leanings, when the rubber meets the road, so to
speak, we will hearken back to what is familiar.

I remember when my son had surgery on his spine. He was only eigh-
teen months old and needed corrective surgery for congenital scoliosis.
For days following the surgery, his mother and I would sit by his hospital bed as he recovered. Sitting at his bedside I would stroke his hair and
softly sing "As the Deer,"[3] a Scripture song from the early 1980s. You see, I
was raised on traditional hymns and praise choruses. As I sat there crying
out to God for healing for my son, the song of my heart was inextricably
linked to my culture.

As defined earlier, worship is our response to the ways God reveals
himself. God shows and tells what He is like, and humans respond with acts
of worship. Because worshipers are so different culturally, our responses,
or acts of worship, will be different as well. How then do we lead worship
with a multi–cultural focus? How do we encourage authenticity among the
varying cultures within our worship services? I believe the answer lies in
convergence worship.

3. "As the Deer" Martin Nystrom ©1984 Universal Music.

Convergence Worship

Convergence worship is celebrating God in a manner reflective of local traditions expressed in ways relevant to the contemporary worshiper. Or as Constance Cherry defines it in her masterful book, "The Worship Architect,"

> Convergence worship is the combining of the historical and the contemporary at every level of worship to create maximum opportunities for engaging worshipers with the presence of God.[4]

Just as God is the same yesterday, today and forever, our worship must be a reflection of tradition while maintaining contemporary relevance all the while being offered by worshipers from varying cultures.

Convergence worship is not what has been termed blended worship. Blended worship attempts to meet a quota: two hymns, two praise choruses, and so on. It is a checklist to cover the bases in an attempt to keep people happy. Convergence worship, by contrast, attempts to glorify God through worship elements that offer unique opportunities for the congregation to meet with God regardless of style.[5]

In order for a congregation to offer authentic worship to God, they must be allowed to respond to his revelations in styles that come naturally to them. Yet, there must be a corporate understanding of worship and the congregation must be encouraged to join with their brothers and sisters in glorifying God, some of whom may have a different culture with a different style.

4. Cherry, The Worship Architect, 248.

5. Tips for offering a convergent worship service: Begin by determining the Scripture passage for the service; consider which worship elements would enhance the passage (regardless of style); be insistent on the use of various art forms as vehicles for worship; consider which songs support the words and theme of the Scripture passage (again, regardless of style)—for instance, if the Scripture passage focuses on the grace of God, you may want to include John Newton's "Amazing Grace" (hymn), Chris Tomlin's "Your Grace Is Enough" (praise chorus), and/or the choral anthem "Amazing Grace" (by Bradley Knight/Geron Davis); be sure to include opportunities for prayer, Scripture reading (responsively, together in unison, etc.), communion, baptism, and other acts of worship when appropriate; encourage congregational participation; expect God to do something in the gathering. For more on convergence worship, see Appendix 3 and I highly recommend chapter 14 of "The Worship Architect" by Constance Cherry.

Multi–Ethnic Worship

Multi-ethnic worship is also critically important in offering authentic worship. A number of years ago I was in Russia worshiping at a church in a city just outside of Moscow. The pews were packed with worshipers excited to worship God. Following the sermon, the congregation began to sing a hymn. Although I was unfamiliar with the words they sang, I recognized the hymn tune. The song was "How Great Thou Art."[6] My team and I began singing the hymn in English as they sang in Russian. We raised our voices together, singing the same song at the same time, but in different languages. At that moment I thought to myself, this is what it will be like when we get to heaven.

Heaven is going to be a wonderful gathering of redeemed worshipers from every tribe, nation and tongue joining together to worship God (see Rev 7:9). I'm not sure if we will all be singing different languages or if there will be one heavenly language, but I do believe that no matter the language, we will understand each other and we will worship together in unity. If this is what we have to look forward to, and yes I am looking forward to that day, than we might as well get used to it here on earth. That is why I am a firm believer in multi-ethnic worship.

Multi-ethnic worship ultimately encourages unity in the body of Christ as we utilize a variety of styles from various people groups. It is in our differences that we find our unity because what we have in common, redemption through the blood of Christ, is greater than all of our differences.

There is evidence throughout Scripture that God desires for our worship to be multi-ethnic. Not only does John's revelation show us an image of multi-ethnic worship in heaven, we see Jesus shattering the preconceived ideas of worship as he speaks with a woman of mixed race at the well (John 4); we see the disciples instructed to share the salvation story with people of every nationality (Matt 28:19); and we see God drawing all believers together for worship at Pentecost (Acts 2).

The day of Pentecost symbolizes unity in the Spirit transcending racial, national and linguistic barriers. The kingdom of God is reinforced by the blessing of Pentecost, seen by scholars from early times as a deliberate and dramatic reversal of the curse of Babel. At Babel human languages were confused and the nations were scattered. In Jerusalem, on the day of Pentecost, supernatural power swept away the language barrier bringing nations

---

6. "How Great Thou Art" Stuart K. Hine ©1949 and 1953 Stuart K. Hine Trust.

and peoples back together. At Babel, the people tried to lift themselves up but God brought them down; at Pentecost, the people were brought up when God came down.

God desires for the nations that he created to worship him:

> There is none like you among the gods, O Lord, nor are there any works like yours. All the nations you have made shall come and worship before you, O Lord, and shall glorify your name. (Ps 86:8-9)

Not only does God want the nations to worship him, his plan is for them to worship together as they gather before his throne to glorify his name.

When we gather for worship with a congregation filled with people of various ethnicities, we get a glimpse of what worship in heaven will be like. It is a beautiful foreshadowing of every tribe, nation and tongue gathering around the throne and singing, "Holy, holy, holy, is the Lord God Almighty! Worthy is the Lamb!" We can sit back and wait for that day, or we can begin now.

Multi–Generational Worship

In addition to multiple cultures and ethnicities, our congregations should be filled with people of various ages. As we look around the sanctuary on a Sunday morning, the pews should be filled with people from the surrounding community. Since many of us do not live in communities comprised of only one people group, our churches should reflect the considerable variety of people within the community. This includes people of varying ages from multiple generations.

I believe the Lord is pleased when our worship services are filled with worshipers of all ages; grandparents worshiping with grandchildren, parents worshiping with children, aunts and uncles worshiping with nephews and nieces, and friends of all ages joining their hearts in one accord.

I understand there is power in worship experiences that primarily include worshipers of the same age group. For example, worship during a high school summer camp can be a very special time; or worship moments at a young couples retreat can make a lasting impression. I'm not saying these times are worthless or not effective in offering true worship to God. What I am saying is that our regularly scheduled times of corporate worship, that every-Sunday-morning gathering, should be comprised of people from various generations.

Here are five reasons our corporate worship gatherings should include worshipers of all ages:

It's Biblical: We see throughout Scripture that people of all ages gathered together to worship God. All ages were together listening as Joshua renewed the covenant with God (Josh 8:35). Jesus gathered children near to him and they (and the adults surrounding him) listened to his words (Matt 19:13–15). Pentecost turned out just as Joel had foretold: sons and daughters prophesying and old men dreaming dreams (Joel 2:28–29; Acts 2:14–41). In the Bible, God's people have always included all ages in worship.

It's Universal: When we join in multi-generational worship, we offer worship that transcends time. For the younger generation, we join our voices with those who have been singing the song of the redeemed longer than we've been alive. For the older generation, we join with voices that will carry the song long after we are called from this earth. What an honor to be part of a tradition of glorifying God that has stood the test of time.

It is good for us to remember God's actions throughout history. There is a danger in not remembering all God has done for us and throughout all of history. I was watching a television show recently about the shapes of the states of the United States of America. The historian told the host that a specific state has "historical amnesia." The people have forgotten the history of the state and it has affected the way they currently live. That statement got me thinking. I believe the church may have a similar problem. The church has historical amnesia.

There is a danger in not remembering all God has done for us as well as throughout all of history. Nehemiah 9:16–17a states, "But they, our ancestors, became arrogant and stiff-necked, and they did not obey your commands. They refused to listen and failed to remember the miracles you performed among them. They became stiff-necked and in their rebellion appointed a leader in order to return to their slavery." We must understand that worship past is connected to worship present. God is faithful and his grace abounds, but our worship is most powerful when we remember God's mighty acts.

A contemporary praise song written by worship leader Tommy Walker entitled "We Will Remember"[7] challenges worshipers to remember the acts

7. "We Will Remember" Tommy Walker ©2005 Doulos Publishing.

of Christ in our lives and to praise him accordingly. Lyrics such as, "*We will remember the works of Your hands; We will stop and give you praise, for great is Thy faithfulness*" and "*I still remember the day You saved me, the day I heard You call out my name; You said You loved me and would never leave me, and I've never been the same*" bring to our attention the importance of remembering God's saving deeds, both historically and personally. The lyric of the bridge portion of the song, "*Hallelujah, hallelujah, to the one from whom all blessings flow; Hallelujah, hallelujah, to the one whose glory has been shown*" reiterates that our remembrance of all God has done leads to praise.

It's Educational: Multi-generational worship offers worshipers the opportunity to learn from one another. We learn songs of praise that have been passed down from one generation to the next. We also have the opportunity to learn new forms of worship from new generations of worshipers. The songs we sing, the prayers we pray, the words spoken over us in a sermon, all teach us about God and his calling on our lives, no matter our age.

It's Authentic: When we worship with those who are in a different age group than we are, we get a more accurate picture of the body of Christ. The Apostle Paul calls believers the body of Christ—a body made up of older and younger members. Each member of the body is equally important. When we worship together, we worship as a healthy body.

The Apostle Paul also calls the church the family of God and families include people of varying ages. Unless churches make a point of planning inclusive worship services, people at both ends of the age spectrum have the tendency to feel left out.

It's Applicable: Truth is not relative and does not change with the times. God's Word is timeless and applicable to all ages. It is no truer today than it was one thousand years ago and remains the same for ages to come. We see throughout Scripture that when the people of God forgot all that God had done for them, they began to get into serious trouble (just take a look through the prophetic books of the Old Testament to see examples; Jeremiah, Ezekiel, Hosea, just to name a few). The fact that Jesus Christ is the Way, the Truth, and the Life will never change and we must not only remember, but pass that truth on to future generations: "One generation shall commend your works to another, and shall declare your mighty acts" (Ps 145:4).

Multi-generational worship offers us an opportunity to worship in a way pleasing to God. My desire is that we see the Church as God sees her and gather all ages, ethnicities and cultures together to give him the glory due his name.

In summary, the primary purpose of the Congregational Worship Gathering is to respond to all God has revealed of himself as we gather together as the body of Christ.

13

The Festival Worship Gathering

Feel! Touch and see
how gracious the Lord is!
Taste, hear, smell, feel and see
how gracious the Lord is!

MADELEINE L'ENGLE

FESTIVAL WORSHIP IS THE type of gathering that is most often confused with congregational worship. It is what I also call "event worship." This is the worship experience found at camps, conferences and concerts. If Congregational Worship is telling your spouse you love them every day, Festival Worship is the once a year, special anniversary dinner. It is important to have regular, consistent times of celebration, but it is also equally important to have the over the top, high energy, high excitement kind of celebratory worship.

Clark describes the Festival Worship Gathering when he explains,

> . . . there was a celebrity status of platform personalities. At each event, it was likely that the vast majority of the attendees did not know each other, yet shared a common focus that prepared them for a high energy, high adrenaline rush that characterized such gatherings, and may have actually defined them after all was said and done . . . in such gatherings (for the most part), people who have gathered are strangers to each other, and thus have very

little relational baggage. Participants know the celebrity leaders by reputation, adding to the expectancy and energy of the gathered crowd, thus affecting each attendee as well.[1]

This type of worship experience is difficult to maintain without a performance component. The quality of performance from the platform is critically important to this gathering. Furthermore, the performance from the platform is really what matters. If the audience is not fully engaged in what is happening from the platform, it does not affect the artist's performance. Sure, it's always better when the audience is engaged as this adds energy to the room, but it does not ultimately affect what is happening on stage.

The performance mentality is further perpetrated by the fact that leaders of Festival Worship Gatherings generally do not know the "audience" very well. Moreover, the gathered worshipers don't know each other well. This is a special event that attracts people from a variety of backgrounds and situations that have gathered with the intent of worshiping God, and will disperse without ever likely seeing each other again.

Planning Festival Worship is done with a specific demographic in mind. Worship at a Promise Keepers event is planned for men; Women of Faith worship is planned for women; and worship planned at a high school summer camp is planned with sixteen year olds in mind. It's no wonder than that the high school students return from camp wishing the worship at church were more like the worship at camp. At camp, worship was planned specifically for them. But at church, worship must be planned for those in the congregation, which ideally will include people from multiple cultures, ethnicities and age groups. At summer camp, high school students worship alongside other high school students. At church, those same students are required to worship alongside grandmas and grandpas, moms and dads, little brothers and little sisters. The worship gatherings will look and feel different . . . as they should.

I regularly teach at worship conferences. At many of the conferences, I have attendees approach me after I have taught a workshop session and share how frustrated—and sometimes they even use the word depressed—they have been while attending the conference. The reason for their feelings is because each morning and evening of the conference, a professional Worship Artist[2] leads worship and these individuals come to me and say, "I could never lead worship like that" or "I don't have the people or the

1. Clark, *Tune My Heart*, 48.
2. We will look at the role of the Worship Artist in Chapter 17.

budget to pull off anything like that." My answer is always the same. "You don't have to!" You see, a worship conference is a Festival Worship Gathering. Our Sunday morning worship services are Congregational Gatherings. Worship that is led in a Festival Worship Gathering should be different than that of a Congregational Gathering because the primary purposes of the two are different. While the Congregational Gathering facilitates corporate expressions of worship, the primary purpose of the Festival gathering is to encourage personal and lifestyle worship.

I believe confusion occurs when expectations carry over from one type of gathering to another. Each gathering possesses a legitimate contribution to the worshiping life of an individual, but we must not mistake one type for another. The worship experience within the Congregational Gathering is going to be different than the worship experience within a Festival Gathering . . . and that's okay.

14

Leading Worship: The Call of Worship Leadership

There is one body and one Spirit—just as you were called to the one hope that belongs to your call—one Lord, one faith, one baptism, one God and Father of all, who is over all and through all and in all.

EPHESIANS 4:4–6

NOT EVERY PERSON CALLED to worship leadership is called to serve in the same way. There are various roles when it comes to serving in the area of worship. Each role is different, yet specific. The difference is found in the primary focus of the role while the approach to fulfilling the role is accomplished in specific ways.

The title of Worship Leader is most commonly used when it comes to worship leadership. Most people assume that standing in front of people and singing or playing worship music makes a Worship Leader, but there are, in fact, different roles when it comes to worship leadership. Not everyone who is called to worship leadership is called to the role of Worship Leader. How one serves and in which role is determined by the calling received from the Lord. Let's take a moment to consider calling.

The word vocation comes from the Latin word *vocare*, which means "to call" or "to summon." The New Testament reference to calling is clear. The term *ecclesia*, which is translated "church" in the English Bible, means "called out." Followers of Christ are called out from the world to worship God and serve others.

Most Christians distinguish between two callings initiated by God: a "general call" and a "specific call." The general call is given to all who have responded to Christ's salvation to serve others and be Christ's presence in the world. We've all received the call to "Go and make disciple of all nations . . . " (Matt 28:19), to "love the Lord your God with all your heart, mind, soul" (Mark 12:30), and to "love your neighbor as yourself" (Mark 12:31).

The specific call is given to individuals in order to accomplish the general call. Each of us has received a specific call that is different than others around us. Every person has been called by God to fulfill his purposes in this world in specific ways. Each calling is unique to the individual. Specific calls may include music ministry, hospitality, missions, and a multitude of others.

A call to ministry may be experienced in different ways, for each individual will relate to God in a personal manner. The calling may be dramatic, prolonged, or may simply come from a realization that you have a certain skill set—that God has gifted you in a special way—and you should use it for the glory of God.

The Dramatic Call

The call to ministry may be dramatic, like it was for the Apostle Paul on the road to Damascus. Before Paul's conversion, he violently persecuted the church.

> For you have heard of my former life in Judaism, how I persecuted the church of God violently and tried to destroy it. (Gal 1:13)

A dramatic event, however, took place in Paul's life while he traveled to Damascus. Paul—whose name was Saul at this point—encountered the risen Christ. Saul was intent on arresting followers of Christ, taking the prisoners to Jerusalem for questioning and possible execution. But as he walked down the dusty road toward Damascus, the voice of Jesus broke through time and space. A member of the Pharisees and persecutor of the followers of Jesus Christ, Saul came face to face with Jesus himself. All those on the road heard the voice and were astonished by a dazzling light. The light shone so bright, and the voice was so powerful, that it drove Saul to his knees. He was blinded by this experience so the others traveling on the road led Saul by hand to Damascus where he awaited further instructions from God (not to mention a name change to Paul).

From that point on, Paul was a follower of Jesus Christ and a powerful witness of the Most High God. This was clearly a dramatic conversion.

The Prolonged Call

A call to ministry may also be prolonged where you can trace God's calling over a period of time through experiences and preparation. This is the way in which God called me to ministry.

I grew up attending church. It started out with my brother and I hopping on the Sunday School bus that would come around our neighborhood. The bus would take us to church every Sunday morning and Wednesday night. Eventually my parents began attending too and from that point on we regularly attended church as a family. Growing up in the church, I participated in ministry on a regular basis. I sang in the church choir, attended Bible studies, led worship for youth group, participated on leadership teams, and more. All of this gave me a foundation and preparation for my calling to ministry.

I attended public schools growing up. The unified school district in my area had programs with advanced courses of study. Since I was interested in marine science, I decided to attend a local high school that had a marine science program. In addition to the general education requirements, students in the marine science program also took classes in marine biology and oceanography. Being so close to the Pacific Ocean (just a few blocks, in fact), we regularly had field trips out on the Pacific in order to do hands–on research and gain underwater diving experience. It was a great program and at the time I was sure I was going to pursue marine science as a career. But God had other plans for my life.

During high school, in addition to the general education and marine science classes, I participated in choir and orchestra (I also ran cross–country and track. Looking back I don't know how in the world I did all of that). After graduating high school, I attended the local community college. There, I sang in the choir and started taking private voice lessons. My voice teacher, at this secular community college, was a Christian and during a lesson half way through my first year she asked if I had ever considered working at a church.

My first reaction was rather humorous now that I look back on it. As mentioned earlier, I grew up attending a small church with a volunteer music director. When she asked me about considering full–time ministry, my response was, "are there actually churches that pay people to direct music?" Well, we both agreed to pray about whether or not God was calling me to church music and worship ministry. By the end of my first year of college, I knew I was not going to be a marine biologist and that God was in fact calling me into ministry.

Looking back I can see how God had been shaping me and revealing his call on my life over the years. He placed me on a path that would lead me to the outcome he had designed from the beginning. The experience and education I have received over the years has helped me work toward fulfilling his call on my life.

The Realized Call

The calling to ministry may also come in the form of a realization that you have been gifted with a certain skill and should use it for God's glory. Ron Kenoly, an internationally known worship leader and popular recording artist with Integrity Music, experienced this type of calling. Some of Ron Kenoly's most popular worship recordings include "Sing Out," "Mourning Into Dancing," and "Jesus Is Alive." Before becoming a worship leader, Kenoly was a secular musician. He had a successful career singing in nightclubs and had recording contracts with MCA, United Artists, Warner Brothers and A&M. But his success came at a high price and that price was his marriage. He and his wife had a turbulent marriage that resulted in their separation. During the separation, his wife became a Christian and returned to the marriage a new person. Ron, seeing the change in her life, sought that change for himself. He found new life in Christ, but this meant the old life needed to go. He knew that if he was going to follow Christ, he should use his musical talent to bring glory to God rather than to himself. So, without hesitation, he walked away from the secular music business, which included solid offers and potentially lucrative contracts.

Charisma magazine describes an August evening in 1982 as Ron struggled with his decision to leave the secular music industry:

> Evenings in the San Francisco Bay area are notoriously cool, but this summer night was sweltering. With his head bowed and his big shoulders hunched in dejection, Ron Kenoly made his way to the little Foursquare church on the corner of 64th Avenue and Bancroft Boulevard.

Slipping into the empty church, he stepped inside the hushed sanctuary and made his way down the aisle. 'Is God still interested in my music?' he wondered.

Although secular record labels were clamoring for his talent, Christian companies had ignored his requests for an audition. Was it possible that his music career ended the day he rededicated his life to the Lord?

Sitting down at the piano, Kenoly began playing the few worship choruses he knew. Surrounded by empty pews in the deserted church, he offered up to God the music that was in his heart.

When the 'concert' was over, a new man emerged from a pool of tears. From that night on Ron Kenoly knew that he was called to perform for an audience of one—God and God alone.[1]

Kenoly states that the summer of 1982 "was a real low point in my life. I couldn't go back to singing secular music even if it meant never singing again."[2] Eventually, the Lord opened the door for Ron to lead worship at Jubilee Christian Center in San Jose, California. His style of worship leading and his ministry with Pastor Dick Bernal led to an invitation to record praise and worship albums with Integrity Music.

The circumstances surrounding your calling by God may not be as interesting as Ron Kenoly's, but God has called you nonetheless. You may quite possibly be reluctant about the calling you have received. But be encouraged! Look throughout Scripture. God regularly called less-prominent and even reluctant individuals to accomplish great things in his name. Like Moses, who received his call to be a critical part of the deliverance of the people of Israel from the grasps of Pharaoh and Egypt. Or David, the shepherd boy turned king, called to be "a man after God's own heart." Esther received her call "for such a time as this" to protect her people from destruction and annihilation. Paul received his call while traveling on a dirt road. His calling led him to be one of the greatest witnesses of the gospel. And God is calling you and me, probably the least obvious of all.

The call of a leader of worship is a privilege that cannot be taken lightly. The Bible tells us that a leader called by God will be held to a high standard according to how they handle the calling (see Jas 3:1; Luke 12:48; Titus 1:7–9).

1. Kenoly and Bernal, *Lifting Him Up*, 11–12.
2. Ibid., 55.

Not many of you should presume to be teachers, my brothers,
because you know that we who teach will be judged more strictly.
(Jas 3:1)

It is an honor to lead God's people in worship and leaders of worship must
be faithful in what God desires for them to do.

The primary question to ask by those being called to worship leadership should be: Which worship leadership role—Worship Leader, Song
Leader, Worship Artist, or Worship Pastor—is God calling me to fulfill?[3]
Each of these roles is a specific worship leadership role of which God calls
people. Understanding God's call is of vital importance in order to successfully fulfill that call.

---

3. This question is of vital importance in understanding, and eventually fulfilling,
your calling. When determining your involvement in a worship position at a church
or ministry organization, it is important for you to ask a secondary question: Which
role—Worship Leader, Song Leader, Worship Artist, or Worship Pastor—is the church
or ministry organization seeking? This is an important question to ask in order to determine whether or not you are a proper fit for the position based on your call by God.

PART FOUR
Roles of Worship Leadership

We must never rest until everything inside us worships God.

A. W. TOZER

THROUGHOUT THE NEXT FOUR chapters, I'd like to over generalize in order to make the distinction between each of these worship leadership roles— Worship Leader, Song Leader, Worship Artist, and Worship Pastor—in a clear and precise manner. I will speak in broad strokes swinging the pendulum far to one side in order to make my point. I understand there are exceptions to every rule and there are some who serve in multiple roles and effectively transition between roles within a given context. As is frequently the case, we should find a middle ground (balance) once we have a clear understanding of both sides. I will, therefore, spend the next four chapters laying out the general characteristics of each worship leadership role and how God can use those called to each role.

* At the conclusion of each of the next four chapters, I will show how each worship leadership role is related to the practice and gathering of worship; as well as sum up the primary responsibility of the role.

15

Worship Leader

. . . set the Levites [worship leaders] apart from the rest of the people of Israel, and the Levites will belong to me. After this, they may go into the Tabernacle to do their work, because you have purified them and presented them as a special offering.

NUMBERS 8:14–15

THE PRIMARY RESPONSIBILITY OF the Worship Leader is to lead the congregation in *their* worship of God. If the congregation, under the leadership of the Worship Leader, does not engage with God in corporate worship, the Worship Leader has failed at their job. Yes, I know that is a bold statement so let me explain.

We must first establish that the Worship Leader's primary job is to lead the congregation in *their* worship of God. When a church invites someone to be a Worship Leader, they are asking that person to stand before the congregation and guide them, to lead them to a place where they can experience the fullness of God. The Worship Leader is not an entertainer, a performer, or a cheerleader. It is not the job of the Worship Leader to model worship, although that is a common practice among today's Evangelical leaders.[1] Nor is it the Worship Leader's job to simply lead music, or to even perform to the best of their ability as a way to encourage others toward

1. See Appendix 5 for the article" Worship Leader vs. Lead Worshiper."

worship.[2] The Worship Leader's job is to lead and instruct the congregation in their worship as they journey together to the throne offering their responses to God's revelations.

Let's take a moment and compare the Worship Leader role to a tour guide. Imagine hiring a tour guide to take you on a tour of the Grand Canyon. As you arrive at the ranger station, the guide says, "Welcome," and then just starts walking. You're not sure if you should follow, but you do—after all, you've already paid for the tour. Each step you take is one of hesitation because you're still not really sure if you should in fact be following or if you should have stayed behind. As you hesitantly walk, you observe many beautiful plants and a few animals scurrying about, but you don't know their names, or even if they are safe. Could they potentially be dangerous or poisonous? The tour guide occasionally looks back to "check in on you," but again, says nothing. Pretty soon, you arrive at your destination. The tour guide stops and stands looking out over the Grand Canyon. They have their back to you and they don't say anything. They are simply standing there admiring the view, and in fact, are in your way, obstructing you from a full view of this majestic place.

I would guess you would say this person was not a very good tour guide. They did not adequately fulfill their responsibilities as a guide. They are not very good at their job. In fact, they have failed to perform the duties of their job.

The same is true of Worship Leaders. It is not enough to stand in front of a congregation and worship, checking in on them occasionally to see if they are okay. Leading corporate worship is a time to be a true leader helping the congregation along the journey of ultimately arriving at the destination while understanding what they are seeing and hearing along the way.

For the Worship Leader, the congregation's experience of worship is their primary responsibility. A Worship Leader is not "successful" in their job if the congregation does not worship.[3] Of course, the goal is to get to the point where the Worship Leader can join the congregation in worship, even as they are leading them. The Worship Leader should declare to the congregation, "Oh, magnify the Lord *with me*, and let *us* exalt his name

2. These are the responsibilities of the Song Leader (see chapter 16) and Worship Artist (see chapter 17) respectively.

3. This is what I call a "Big Picture" statement. There will be times when individuals in the congregation struggle to worship due to circumstances beyond the Worship Leader's control. The Worship Leader must simply provide the best opportunities for them to worship and pray the congregation experiences God in a fresh, new way.

together" (Ps 34:3). This is much like the tour guide. Though there is a job that must be done in order to assist others in experiencing the journey, the guide, or in this case, the Worship Leader, also gets to enjoy the beauty and majesty along the way.

Jim Altizer shares a great analogy of a Worship Leader:

> The Worship Leader is like the Palm Sunday donkey. The Palm Sunday donkey? That's right! A Worship Leader has the same job that the Palm Sunday donkey had. His job was to deliver Jesus to the people. No one recalls the donkey's training or lineage. No one knows if he ever carried another VIP, or whether he got big and strong. This donkey merely delivered the Messiah to his worshipers and then sank back into obscurity.
>
> Yes! The donkey was at the celebration. He heard the shouts of "Hosanna in the highest!" but never thought the people were yelling for him. He stepped on the palms and cloaks, which had been spread out for the Christ, but drew no personal honor from it. The donkey was center stage and was serving Jesus in his area of giftedness, but never expected special treatment. Though Isaiah had prophesied his presence that day, the donkey's name is not even recorded. He was just able, available, and privileged to be used; it was all about Jesus![4]

Mature Worship Leaders must manage stylistic preference and comfort with the needs of both the community and the mission of the church. Again, it is not about the Worship Leader and what they like or how they are "performing." Since it is about the congregation, worship leading should be done in a way that encourages corporate response to God. Worship Leaders, therefore, should provide numerous and diverse ways to express worship and avoid being preoccupied with personal preference.

John the Baptist: The Worship Leader's Role Model

Worship Leaders should strive to deflect attention away from them and onto God. God is the Object and Subject of our worship, not the Worship Leader and/or team. John the Baptist tells us "The Bride belongs to the Bridegroom" (John 13:29). Worship Leader David Ruis says, "The Bride is the Bridegroom's and his alone. Attracting attention to ourselves and away from Christ is as offensive as a best man flirting with his friend's bride as

4. Jim Altizer. "3 Profiles of A Worship Leader." *Roadmaps for Worship*. http://roadmapsforworship.com/?page_id=354

she comes up the aisle."[5] The Baptizer provided us with an example for how to deflect attention to the One who truly deserves it when he said: "He must increase but I must decrease" (John 3:30). Almighty God—Father, Son, and Holy Spirit—is the only one worthy of praise and worship. The Worship Leader must lead the congregation in their worship of the Bridegroom, and not flirt with his bride.

Leading the Congregation's Worship

When planning a worship service, a Worship Leader sees worship as more than just the songs that are sung. They plan the service with the non-musical portions in mind. They plan the times in between the songs. What prayers will be used in the worship service and where will they be placed? What Scripture passages will be read in the service? Will there be any other worship elements utilized (silence, communion, baptism, multi-media, dance, etc.) and when will they occur in the service? The Worship Leader desires to lead the congregation not only in singing songs, but also through the other elements of the worship service. These other elements are just as important to the Worship Leader as the songs. In fact, during the week, the Worship Leader spends quality time preparing prayers, Scripture readings and other worship elements, not just practicing and preparing the songs. The flow of the service and the transitions between elements is important to the Worship Leader because these affect the focus of the content of the service and ultimately the avenue of worship for the congregation.

Throughout my years of ministry, I have had the privilege of working with two men that epitomize the qualities of a Worship Leader. They have developed ways in which to encourage the congregation to full participation in worship.

Dr. Jim Altizer, Coordinator of the Master of Arts in Pastoral Studies Worship Leadership emphasis at Azusa Pacific University, has an incredible gift of leading congregational worship. He possesses a remarkable ability to lead a congregation into the very presence of God. In an article entitled "Look, Ma, No Congregation!" Jim says,

> Worship leaders can lead and prompt, but until corporate participation is a priority, we have only entertained. Worship must be varied and creative if people are to experience fresh and mature

5. David Ruis, quoted by Tom Kraeuter in *Developing an Effective Worship Ministry*, 12.

worship. Truth must precede response if it is to be assumed that the Holy Spirit is engaging people's emotions. To that end, worship leaders must discern whether their people love "worship," or the Living God. Neither should we addict our people to our particular style of worship leading, nor to the warm feelings that come through repetition or ascending key-changes.

If the worship service could not proceed without the congregation, we must be sure that we are utilizing a variety of worship tools in order to keep response fresh, balanced, and mature. The alternative is either mindless liturgy or emotional addiction. If the congregation is a nice addition but unnecessary to the service, then the worship leader and the pastor must lead toward change, for if a people's appreciation of change grows stale, they will soon only appreciate stale things.[6]

To accomplish congregational participation in worship, Jim has developed a pattern for planning and leading worship that incorporates frames of reference as a way of lending meaning to and renewing significance of worship. He calls his method *Roadmaps for Worship*™.[7] There are three roadmap options that Jim uses when planning worship services; each saturated with Scripture.

One type of roadmap is *topical worship*. Topical worship uses a theme, such as the attributes of God, to unify a package of songs. The focus on an attribute of God, such as his holiness, provides the foundation for the selection of songs and Scripture passages to be used in the worship service.

A second type of roadmap is *verse worship*. Verse worship not only leads people in worship, but also teaches them how to use Scripture for worship in their own devotional times. An example of this type of roadmap would be Isaiah 6, which provides verse-by-verse instruction for entering the presence of God: verses 1 and 2 = his presence, verse 3 = his worship, verses 4 and 5 = our unworthiness, verses 6 and 7 = cleansing.

A third type of roadmap is called *pathway worship*. Pathway worship provides the worshiper with a map or blueprint for worship. The use of acronyms like A.C.T.S. (adoration; confession; thanksgiving; supplication), and designs like the layout of the temple (outer court, inner court, holy of holies) provide Scripture-based guidance for both corporate and individual worship.

6. Jim Altizer. "Look, Ma, No Congregation!" *Roadmaps for Worship*. http://roadmapsforworship.com/?page_id=369

7. See Appendix 6 for a sample Roadmap for Worship.

Roadmaps for Worship™ are theological roadmaps that help keep the main thing the main thing. It turns an audience back into a congregation, equipping them to worship God in and through authentic expressions. Using a roadmap in congregational worship encourages worshipers to stop ignoring each other and start experiencing God in, with, and through others.

The other Worship Leader I have an enormous amount of respect for is Walt Harrah. Walt is the Elder of Worship at Grace Evangelical Free Church in La Mirada, California. He is a gifted musician and songwriter, with numerous songs published including "No More Night"[8] and the praise songs "Think About His Love"[9] and "Here Is Your God."[10] The thing that impresses me most about Walt, however, is his passion for leading God's people in worship.

Each week Walt creates a Worship Script[11] that knits together Scripture, prayer, theological quotes, and songs. The cohesive incorporation of various elements within the script provides a powerful opportunity for the congregation to respond to God in worship. In reference to the development of Worship Scripts, Walt says,

> The truth about God registers in the head first, and we were created to respond to truth in some emotive way. Thus the Bible instructs us to sing, clap, pray, dance, shout, to confess, to give thanks, to rejoice.
>
> But those actions are based on who God is, and are in response to what we know to be true about God, and what he has done. That's why the mind is so important. It comprehends to some degree the greatness of God, and his goodness. To leave our minds out in the foyer of the church makes no sense at all.
>
> So the worship of God must make room for both the head and the heart in order to have maximum impact, and to glorify God, instead of merely giving us a worship buzz. A major problem we face today is that worship has become a synonym for singing. And if we stop and think about God by reading a portion of scripture, or making a God–focused comment, or praying, that can be seen as disturbing the "flow" of worship, and is often avoided as disruptive to worship.

---

8. "No More Night" Walt Harrah ©1984 Word Music, Inc.

9. "Think About His Love" Walt Harrah ©1987 Integrity's Hosanna! Music.

10. "Here Is Your God" Walt Harrah ©2010 SeedSower Music.

11. See Appendix 7 for a sample Worship Script.

I argue that those moments of not singing are opportunities—pit stops—to fuel the mind with additional information with which we can then turn into even greater praise.

The worship scripts . . . are my attempts at engaging the head and the heart around a single focused aspect of God's character. The songs are placed in a way to help the heart respond to the input that the mind has just received.[12]

As Walt leads the congregation through the Worship Script, they are encouraged to join with those around them in offering worship to God. Participation of the congregation is the main concern for Walt as a Worship Leader. The congregation could potentially be tempted to focus on something other than God, such as the musicianship of those leading in musical worship. The worship team is composed of high quality musicians. Walt himself is a sought after session singer and has earned respect in the music industry. Although he is concerned with the quality of musicianship, with the desire to offer the most excellent musical effort as possible, Walt's primary focus is on the congregation and their participation in worship. It is this focus on the congregation that makes Walt an effective Worship Leader.

The Worship Leader must never forget that there is a congregation out there and that it is the Worship Leader's responsibility to lead that congregation in experiencing the fullness of being in God's presence. Leading congregational worship is not about the Worship Leader and how good they or the band sound.[13] If mistakes are made in the worship service—and mistakes will be made on occasion—the Worship Leader has the ability to recover quickly because they know it is not about what is happening on the platform, but what is happening in the congregation that matters.[14]

Leading worship is also not about how well the Worship Leader worships. It is about the congregation's experience as they come before God. Worship Leaders should join them on the journey, as part of the body of

12. Walt Harrah. "Worship Scripts." *Seedsower Music.* http://www.waltharrah.com/worship_script_intro

13. This is not an excuse for poor musicianship. We should always strive to offer God our most excellent effort. God deserves nothing less than our best. We must not, however, make it about our efforts, but maintain the focus on the congregation's efforts in worshiping the one true God.

14. This is not an excuse to be sloppy or careless. Mistakes can be distracting. We should do everything in our power to minimize distractions in a worship service. We don't want to do or say anything that takes attention away from God—good or bad. The focus should stay on God. Mistakes, however, should not "make or break" a worship service.

Christ, but must not get lost in worship and leave the congregation behind. There is an old saying, "If you think you're leading but no one is following you, then you're only taking a walk." If the congregation is left behind, the Worship Leader has not fulfilled their responsibility to lead worship.

The mandate of the Worship Leader is to lead the congregation through expressions and experiences that will immerse them into the very being of God. As the Worship Leader is leading worship, if the congregation is not engaged in the actions of worship, the Worship Leader should be willing and able to be flexible and change what is being done in order to usher the people more effectively into a spirit of worship, praise and thanksgiving toward God.

Worship Role: Worship Leader

Worship Type: Corporate

Worship Gathering: Congregational; Family

Primary Responsibility: To lead the congregation in *their* worship

16

Song Leader

Great theology, married to great hymnology,
rises to God in great doxology.

STEPHEN OLFORD

THE SONG LEADER HAS similarities to the Worship Leader. They are both primarily concerned with worship within the context of a congregational gathering. They also share in the desire to lead the congregation in worship. The most significant difference between the two roles is that a Song Leader is predominantly concerned with the songs of the worship service while a Worship Leader is concerned with every element of worship in the service, not just the music.

My wife and I serve in worship ministry together. We have led worship together in various ministry settings such as churches, retreats, and camps. She has also been by my side for the nearly two decades that I have served in full-time church ministry. There was a period of time when I was not serving at a church in a full-time capacity. During this time we led worship at various churches, filling in for worship leaders on vacation or helping churches in transition. I remember preparing to lead Sunday services at a particular church. We had never been to this church before, so like I do every time I lead at a new place, I set up a meeting with the senior pastor to learn about the church and get all of the pertinent information needed to effectively lead the congregation in worship (Scripture text, sermon theme, list of songs the church knows, etc.). As I spoke with the pastor he said these words to me, "Don't talk too much in between songs. Let me do the preaching and you do the singing." It was clear to me this pastor wanted a Song Leader to focus on leading the music in the worship services . . . and nothing more.

There is nothing wrong with being a Song Leader in a church. The role of Song Leader is a specific calling by God and there are many churches looking for someone called to serve in this role. There is also some cross-over between Song Leaders and Worship Leaders as Song Leaders generally lead in the worship that occurs in the midst of songs. The focus of a Song Leader, however, is to lead the musical portions of the service, and let others lead the other elements of worship.

A Song Leader's primary responsibility is to lead the congregation in their song. Congregational song is, as Brian Wren points out, "anything that the worshiping congregation sings, not as presentation or performance to someone else, but as a vehicle for its encounter with God."[1] The Song Leader, then, is not performing music for the congregation, but encouraging the congregation to sing out praises to God.

Sing to the Lord!

Throughout Scripture, the command to sing is given to God's people over four hundred times. This is not an option nor is it a recommendation. It is a command appropriate for everyone. There are no requirements for singing other than having a song to sing. And all Christians have a song to sing—it is the song of the redeemed, sung by everyone who has been redeemed by Christ. Isaac Watts said, "Let those refuse to sing who never knew our God."[2] Those who are redeemed know God so we must not refuse to sing! There are no prerequisites to sing this song; other than to accept the redemption freely offered by God. When that occurs, God simply says, "Sing!"

In the Old Testament we see that singing was an important mandated element of worship in the temple. The Levites were instructed to lead the people in song and furthermore, the people were expected to join in the singing. There are numerous psalms that command the worshiper to sing: "Oh sing to the Lord a new song; sing to the Lord, all the earth! Sing to

1. Wren, *Praying Twice*, 2.
2. "Marching to Zion" Isaac Watts, Public Domain, 1707.

the Lord, bless his name; tell of his salvation from day to day" (Ps 96:1–2). This command does not change in the New Testament. The Apostle Paul encouraged the New Testament church to sing (see 1 Cor 14:26; Eph 5:19; Col 3:16). Worshipers have no option but to sing because Scripture commands it. Week after week, gathered as the body of Christ, we are spiritually renewed, realigned, and sanctified by singing to the Lord and singing to one another. "The crucial question is not 'Do you have a voice?' but 'Do you have a song?'"[3] As redeemed people, the answer is always, "Yes!"

Stop Believing the Lie

I believe one the greatest lies the evil one has convinced us to buy into is that we "can't sing." Over the years I have heard countless Christians say they can't sing. Either they were told so at a young age or they just don't feel confident when they sing. My response is always the same: "That is a lie from the pit of hell." The evil one knows the power of singing God's praises, so he has convinced us that we can't, or shouldn't sing. We must stop believing that lie! When we buy into the lie that we can't sing or our voices are a hindrance to our worship, Satan is victorious.

We have a problem in our churches that I call the American Idol Syndrome. Because of our culture's obsession with "reality" singing competitions, our congregations come to the worship service with two preconceived ideas: 1) they expect the worship team singers to sound like the latest competitors on television; and 2) they feel minimized because they don't sound like the latest competitors on television.[4] As those who lead the congregation's song, we must instruct and encourage the congregation to use their voices, however they sound, for the glory of God. After all, God is not listening to the pitch or tone quality as much as he is listening to the heart.[5]

3. Hustad, *Jubilate II*, 448.

4. Furthermore, members of the congregation can often have an attitude of critiquing the "performance" of the worship team just as a judge on the show would do. Does the worship team deserve a golden ticket to Hollywood?

5. I appreciate the fact that American Idol and other similar shows provide an opportunity for singers to break into the music business. I am not saying that these shows are inherently wrong. The issue is when Christians bring the singing competition mentality into a worship service. Our worship services should not look, feel, or be critiqued like a reality television show.

Singing God's Story

The Song Leader understands that congregational song is the heart and soul of all worship music.[6] As we gather for worship, the songs we sing help to remind us of the story of God. We remember all God has done for us in the past, recall the blessings he has permitted for us in the present, and anticipate all that God has promised to accomplish in the future. Singing the story of God not only joins us with the redeemed in our local gathering, but also with those spread out around the globe. Moreover, as we sing, we join with the saints of old and the heavenly hosts praising God.

Singing in Community

Singing is an important aspect of communal worship as it has the power to unite groups of people. Even within secular settings, singing has the powerful affect of uniting people: strangers sing together as they gather to remember a loved one at a memorial service or fans sing "Sweet Caroline" at a Red Sox game. Within the Church, singing together is the quickest way to unite a gathering of individuals, no matter how large or small, into one corporate worshiping body; the body of Christ. John Chrysostom (380 AD) notes the unique way in which singing together brings a diverse group of individuals together in unity:

> The psalm which occurred just now in the office [worship service] blended all voices together, and caused one single fully harmonious chant to arise; young and old, rich and poor, women and men, slaves and free, all sang one single melody. . . . All the inequalities of social life are here banished. Together we make up a single choir in perfect equality of rights and of expression whereby earth imitates heaven. Such is the noble character of the Church.[7]

Marva Dawn states, "We don't go to church, we are the church and go to worship to learn how to be the church."[8] The responsibility of the Song Leader is to help people express the community that already exists. Dietrich

6. I am deeply indebted to Constance Cherry for influencing my thoughts on much of the material in this chapter. Her book "The Worship Architect" and her classes on congregational song at Azusa Pacific University and The Robert E. Webber Institute for Worship Studies were invaluable to me.

7. Webber, *Worship Old and New*, 176.

8. Dawn, *A Royal "Waste" Of Time*, 256-257.

Bonhoeffer understood the importance of how the personal singing voice joins with the voice of the singing community,

> The more we sing, the more joy we will derive from it, but, above all, the more devotion and discipline and joy we put into our singing, the richer will be the blessing that will come to the whole life of the fellowship from singing together. It is the voice of the Church that is heard in singing together. It is not you that sings, it is the Church that is singing, and you, as a member of the Church, may share in its song. Thus all singing together that is right must serve to widen our spiritual horizon, make us see our little company as a member of the great Christian Church on earth, and help us willingly and gladly to join our singing, be it feeble or good, to the song of the Church.[9]

Singing Songs that Teach

We sing because it is a way for us to express our faith. Much of our theology is received and expressed through the songs we sing. The words of songs can instruct and teach us. Lyrics such as "O worship the King, all glorious above and gratefully sing His wonderful love" instruct us to worship. "Take time to be holy, speak oft with thy Lord" encourages our daily disciplines. The lyrics "share His love by telling what the Lord has done for you" teach us how to share the love of God with others. This is why John Wesley was so adamant when it came to singing songs exactly as they were written: "Sing them exactly as they are printed here, without altering or mending them at all; and if you have learned to sing them otherwise, unlearn it as soon as you can."[10]

I believe Wesley's goal with his statement was to encourage worshipers to maintain the purity of the doctrine contained in the hymns. I don't believe Wesley would argue with slight lyrical alterations as a result of changes in the vernacular as the centuries have passed. There are certain non–essential words that are no longer in use and others that may potentially cause confusion or misinterpretation. Words found in traditional hymns like *fetter, welkin,* or *hasten* can appropriately be translated today as *chain, heaven,* and *hurry* without harming the doctrinal intent of the hymn. William Cowper's "My Bowels Yearn O'er Dying Men" is a powerful

9. Bonhoeffer, *Life Together*, 61.

10. From Sacred Melody, 1761, quoted in preface to *The Methodist Hymnal* (1964), viii. See Appendix 10 for the complete list of "Directions for Singing" by John Wesley.

hymn when you consider the word *bowels* in Cowper's day meant the same as when we talk about the heart—that deep-seated place within you where your passions and integrity reside. Singing, "my heart aches for dying men" would be more fitting today. There are also words of which perspectives have changed over the years—such as awful, which when originally written would have meant to inspire reverential wonder (as in awesome or full of awe), but today is generally interpreted as meaning very bad or unpleasant. If changes are made, not simply for clarity, but to change the context or content of the song, especially to make it mean something other than it intended, the hymn has been hijacked and essentially ruined.

One example that gets to the heart of Wesley's concern is the Presbyterian Church (USA)'s rejection of the modern hymn "In Christ Alone"[11] in their hymnal. The reason for its rejection was because the songwriters, Keith Getty and Stuart Townend, refused to allow a line in their song to be changed. The lyrics in question are written,

> *Till on that cross as Jesus died*
> *The wrath of God was satisfied*

The hymn committee wanted to change the lyrics to,

> *Till on that cross as Jesus died*
> *The love of God was magnified*

After the songwriters did not allow their lyrics to be changed, the committee voted to not include the song in their hymnal. For Getty and Townend, and a host of others who responded through media outlets, the word changes were not simple vernacular changes but significant doctrinal changes. We must be careful of this in our churches as well. The songs we sing teach theology so we must take care to sing songs with correct and meaningful theological truths and not shy away from those truths that might make us feel uncomfortable.

The great creeds of the Christian faith, such as the Nicene and Apostles' creeds, provide an avenue for teaching essential doctrine and concepts of the faith. Barry Liesch suggests that, "some churches might prefer to sing a creed rather than read it. A paraphrased version of the Apostles' Creed can be sung to the hymn of 'Glorious Things of Thee Are Spoken' (Austrian Hymn)."

The Apostles' Creed *(paraphrased)*

---

11. "In Christ Alone" Keith Getty and Stuart Townend ©2001 Thankyou Music.

I believe in God the Father, Maker of the heaven and earth,
And in Jesus Christ, our Savior, God's own Son of matchless worth;
By the Holy Ghost conceivéd, Virgin Mary bore God's Son,
He in whom I have believéd, God Almighty, Three in One.

Suffered under Pontius Pilate, crucified for me He died
Laid within the grave so silent, gates of Hell He opened wide.
And the stone-sealed tomb was empty, on the third day He arose,
Into heaven made His entry, Mighty Conqueror of His foes.

At God's right hand He is seated, till His coming, as He said,
Final judgment will be meted to the living and the dead,
I confess the Holy Spirit has been sent through Christ the Son,
To apply salvation's merit, God the Spirit—Three in One.

I believe that all believers form one body as a whole.
We are one throughout the ages, with the saints I lift my soul.
I believe sins are forgiven, that our bodies will be raised,
Everlasting life in heaven, Amen, let His name be praised![12]

Our singing also has the potential of teaching us how to pray more effectively. Much of our worship singing is prayer that directly addresses God. Worshipers sing words of praise, lament, confession, thanksgiving, and proclamation to God through sung prayers. Augustine has been attributed to saying, "he who sings prays twice." Spurgeon tells us that, "God is to be praised with the voice, and the heart should go therewith in holy exultation."[13] Singing is a powerful way of communicating with God in ways that reveal who God is and who we are in light of his revelation. Our prayerful songs are spiritually formative for our lives.

Singing Songs that Form Us

Because of the spiritually formative value of the words of our worship, Song Leaders must pay attention to song selection. There is an adaptation to the Latin phrase *lex orandi, lex credendi* = the way in which we worship is the way in which we believe; that states *lex cantandi, lex credendi* = the way in which we sing is the way in which we believe. People form the words and

---

12. Liesch, *People In the Presence of God*, 107–108.
13. Spurgeon, *The Treasury of David*, 108.

the words form the people. The songs we sing in church embed themselves into our minds as truth. I have had conversations with people about faith and they begin, without realizing, to quote song lyrics as a defense for what they believe. The words of hymns and worship songs sung over the years have become an important part of their belief system. Plato once said, "Let me write the songs of a nation, and I care not who writes its laws." He understood the power of songs to shape the beliefs and lives of people.

The songs we choose for our congregation will help them live well or conversely, not live well. A student in one of my worship ministry classes shared that his worship mentor would encourage the worship leaders at his church to sing songs that people could die to. In other words, sing songs that help us live, and die, well. Songs filled with good and accurate theology; songs that draw us closer to God rather than farther away; songs that we can sing on our death beds and feel the presence of God drawing near. Song Leaders, are you teaching songs that can be sung around a hospital bed in 50 years?

The songs we choose for our congregation, as well as the songs that we withhold from them, are a significant component to their spiritual development.

Singing Songs with Jesus

When Christians gather we become the very body of Christ and our communal expression becomes the very breath of the living God. Congregational singing is seen then to be the living voice of Christ in our midst. The Song Leader must encourage the congregation to follow Jesus as the ultimate Song Leader. As our attention is focused on Jesus, we join him in song. Jesus is the primary Song Leader, ministering on our behalf, declaring to the Father, "in the midst of the congregation I will sing your praise" (Heb 2:12). He is our Great High Priest interceding for us as we approach the throne of grace. Reggie Kidd states, concerning Jesus,

> . . . there is only one priestly order that could establish a permanently "new song," only one director who could incorporate into a single choir people of every race and nation, tribe and tongue, bandwidth and skill–level, only one singer who could lead that menagerie into the fray against the powers and principalities: he who went all the way into the silence of sin–forsakenness and rose in victory to be God–incarnate singing over his people with love

(Zeph 3:17). The glory of song in worship is that we get to join our voices to his. His is the voice that counts, not ours.[14]

Leading the Congregation's Song

As we join in congregational singing, some sort of leadership is required, as people don't normally begin singing spontaneously. This leadership, however, should never overshadow the song of the people. The voice of the congregation should be primary for it is the main instrument in congregational song. Christians have inherited the musical tradition of the synagogue in which the gathered assembly is led by one voice, the cantor (or in modern terms, the song leader). Early Christians battled over the inclusion of instruments in the liturgy at all. Organ began accompanying hymns as late as the last half of the sixteenth century. Before that, it would introduce the hymn and play in alternation with the unison, unaccompanied congregation. The term "a cappella" literally means "as in the chapel" and was originally used in reference to congregational singing.

While respectfully acknowledging those few Christian traditions that do not employ singing in their worship, Constance Cherry states, "Christians singing the faith is a necessity for engaging in fully biblical worship."[15] The Song Leader understands that congregational song is indispensible to Christian worship. Christianity is a singing faith. Worshipers sing as a response to who God is and what he has done, is doing and will do.

The church has been singing its praise for longer than its formal existence. Old Testament followers of Yahweh sang praise by means of canticles and psalms. Moses led the people in singing the song of the redeemed. David led the people in singing praise psalms in the presence of the Ark (the place of God's presence on earth). The New Testament church continued those traditions and added hymns and spiritual songs to the repertoire. The church of God has always been a singing faith.

A main responsibility of the Song Leader is to help the congregation find its voice. The Song Leader facilitating the song of the people must take into account a variety of factors:

14. Reggie Kidd. "Jesus Christ, Our Worship Leader." *Worship Leader* (March/April 2011). http://www.mydigitalpublication.com/article/Feature_-_Jesus_Christ,_Our_Worship_Leader/653277/62452/article.html

15. Cherry, *The Worship Architect*, 154.

- Who will make up the gathering?
- What is their age range?
- What are they used to singing in church?
- What part does the music play in the flow of the service?
- How might the Song Leader facilitate not only mood but also flow?
- How musically literate is the congregation?

These questions and more are important to consider when leading a congregation in musical worship. In addition, guidelines for congregational singing help congregations sing well and Song Leaders to lead well. In an effort to strengthen congregational singing in his church, eighteenth century preacher John Wesley wrote his "Directions for Singing."[16] Brian Wren includes his guidelines in his book Praying Twice.[17] Ultimately, in order to effectively lead in congregational song, a Song Leader should sing songs that are familiar, sung more frequently, are sing–able, and can preferably, at any given moment, be sung a cappella.

Sing Songs That Are Familiar

Singing familiar songs means we must teach new songs less frequently. I recommend teaching no more than one to two new songs per month. When a new song is taught, make every effort to sing it again within the next two weeks. Generally, when I teach a new song, I sing it again the very next week, then take the third week off, and sing it again on the fourth week. This allows the congregation to become familiar with the song and fully participate in the worship service. By allowing songs to make their way into the rotation more often the congregation becomes familiar with the songs and are encouraged to sing out. But be careful to not overdo this. Singing the same song six out of eight Sundays may be a bit too much.

Sing Songs That Are Singable

The Song Leader must also choose songs that are singable for the congregation. When considering whether or not a song is appropriate for

16. See Appendix 8.
17. See Appendix 9.

congregational use, think about the melody of the song and whether it is singable for the average church goer (think middle schooler just starting out in band and grandma who has grown up singing from a hymnal). Is the melody crafted in a way that flows well? If you hum the melody, is it beautiful? My good friend Andrew Braine, founder of worshipbetter.com, says, "As a general rule, if most members of your congregation wouldn't ever be caught humming the melody, it probably is not a strong melody." So, hum the melody. Is it beautiful? Is it memorable?

Is the song's melodic range accessible to the congregation? Many melody lines of contemporary praise songs (and some traditional hymns) are in a range too wide for the average congregation member to sing. Ruth King Goddard claims,

> Identifying specific keys will not define whether or not a song has the needed range. The melodic contour in a song can easily be in any key, but still keep within or move beyond a specific vocal range. This is especially true as much of the newer music has a much looser tonal center and creative songwriters are moving past the common melodic templates of the past. So we have to look at the notation of a song or listen and find where the highest and lowest notes lie.[18]

People today have smaller singing vocal ranges than previous generations.[19] There may be a number of reasons for this including the lack of musical

18. Ruth King Goddard, email message to author, July 25, 2014.

19. Ruth King Goddard claims the shrinking vocal range is a result of the demise of the personal singing voice and the cultural immersion in a technologically-driven tonal or "sound ideal." In her paper "Who Gets to Sing in the Kingdom" presented for the Christian Congregational Music Conference at Ripon College in Oxford, United Kingdom, she states, "it's crucial to recognize that those who have had little or no singing training or encouragement usually have little awareness of any range beyond their normal speaking voice. The range limits for a combined adult population would be B up to A. This means that songs that use any notes in the head voice range have limited accessibility. Of course this eliminates most of traditional hymnody, and much of popular contemporary music. Thus the reality of this limitation in ability creates a great need for new songwriting that recognizes this limitation. It is imperative for songwriters who write for the congregation to consider the entire congregation's range, not their own personal range. That doesn't mean the congregation cannot sing songs with a wider range. Some congregations can do more than others. The ranges available to be sung will vary based on the congregation's ability, but at the same time must consider the needs of the most spiritually vulnerable. The prevalence of unchurched adults is one, but not the only factor that may have an effect on the level of participatory song ability in a congregation. For instance, those in their later years have an increasingly difficulty reaching the higher

training in schools, less opportunities to sing in today's culture (a result of being an increasingly non-singing culture), and believing the lie that they can't or shouldn't sing. Regardless, as leaders of worship, we must consider the vocal range of our congregational songs and determine if our people can effectively, and physically, sing the songs.

A common occurrence in modern worship songs is the octave melody jump. Jumping the octave may sound great on a recording and in performance venues, but the average congregation member will not be able to follow along. If our goal in congregational worship is full participation, doing something the congregation cannot do does not help in accomplishing our goal. One must also consider the purpose of the vocal octave jump. Is it to benefit the congregation and their worship or is it primarily to add to the performance of the song?

Sing Songs A Cappella

There is a school of thought that says if you want people to sing louder, turn up the volume of the music. That philosophy may work well in a festival-style event, where the band cranks up the amps and the people practically scream in order to be heard. When it comes to congregational singing, however, the voice of the congregation should be of utmost importance. The congregation should never have to scream in order to be heard (or hear their own voice). We should turn the volume down and encourage the congregation to sing out allowing them the opportunity to fulfill Paul's encouragement to sing to one another (see Eph 5). At least once in the worship service, cut out the band, back away from the microphone and encourage the congregation to sing a cappella. This allows the congregation the chance to hear themselves, be encouraged by their own voices, and encourage others in their worship of God.

If a main responsibility of the Song Leader is to lead the congregation in their song, the congregation should be singing. Ken Read shares this personal story,

> When I visited a monastery a while back, I learned some important lessons from my brothers there about community singing. First of

notes that were easy in their youth. But a church that is reaching the unchurched and is concerned about spiritual formation through worship song must make serious consideration of song accessibility."

all, each member of the community is seen as having a responsibility to the others to help carry the load. They take the principle of sharing seriously. Each member finds his or her own voice—a straight tone, without vibrato or stylistic flair—and blends it with the rest. There is no room for a person singing too softly, and no room for someone to stand out above the others. We are all equal in this work of worship in song.[20]

But what do you do if the congregation does not sing? I encountered this situation at a church after becoming their Worship Pastor. It was a wonderful group of people but they did not participate fully when it came time to sing. I discovered there were a few reasons for this based on their previous experience with worship leaders (particularly style) and the song selection. As a result, I decided to set a goal to have the congregation singing out in full participation within six months. I informed the worship leadership team at the church of my goal and asked them for their help. We decided on a four–fold approach:

1. New Songs

We decided to introduce new songs less frequently. We would teach no more than two new songs per month and when a new song was taught, we made an effort to sing it again within the next two weeks.

2. Song Repertoire

The song repertoire of the church had become too large. The worship leaders in the church had too many songs to choose from. This led to the congregation never really being able to become familiar with any given song. We needed to shorten the repertoire and sing songs more frequently.

20. Read, *Created to Worship*, 232–233.

3. Song Lists[21]

I created three song lists to be used when selecting songs for congregational worship: Top 40, Bottom 60, and Classics.[22] The church selected a theme for the entire church each year. The Top 40 list contained songs that matched the theme for the year as well as any new songs we wanted to teach the congregation. The Bottom 60 list consisted of songs from the previous year that we wanted to have the congregation continue to sing. The Classics list included songs that were so familiar to the church, that when sung, practically everyone joined in because they knew it so well ("Shout to the Lord,"[23] "How Great Is Our God,"[24] and "Open The Eyes of My Heart"[25] were on this list).

Our Worship Leaders would select 50 percent of their songs for any given Sunday from the Top 40 list. The other 50 percent of songs were to be selected from either the Bottom 60 list, Classics list or they could select a hymn.

This process of selecting songs from these organized song lists accomplished a couple of things: 1) the worship leaders were given guidelines for song selection; and 2) songs were being sung more frequently, giving the congregation the opportunity to learn them and participate more fully.

4. A Cappella

At least once in the service, the worship leader was required to cut out the band, back away from the microphone and encourage the congregation to sing a cappella. The purpose was to allow the congregation the chance to hear themselves and be encouraged by their own voices.

---

21. The songs selected to be included on the lists went through the process of a song selection rubric based on "Selecting Worship Songs: A Guide For Leaders" by Cherry, Brown and Bounds. The rubric focused on theological, musical and lyrical considerations for each song. Before making its way onto one of our lists, the song needed to pass the rubric.

22. Worship leaders could also select a hymn as one of their songs. So in essence, there were four lists to choose from.

23. "Shout to the Lord" Darlene Zschech ©1993 Wondrous Worship.

24. "How Great Is Our God" Chris Tomlin, Ed Cash, and Jesse Reeves ©2003 worshiptogether.com songs.

25. "Open the Eyes of My Heart" Paul Baloche ©1997 Integrity's Hosanna! Music.

A decision was made to follow the above guidelines for a six–month period with the hope of accomplishing our goal of encouraging the congregation to participate more fully in singing within the worship services. To our delight we accomplished the goal within three months. Three months! The congregation began singing out in a way they never had before. We were amazed. Moreover, we decided to continue to follow the guidelines beyond the six–month trial period.

Logistically, the Song Leader will spend the majority of their time during the week practicing and rehearsing the music for a worship service. The Song Leader is not primarily concerned with any of the other elements in the service and will leave it to someone else to fill in the "blank" spaces—those elements in the service that are not music. The Song Leader is in charge of the songs and will leave it to someone else to plan and implement the other important worship elements.

With music being the primary focus of the Song Leader, the recovery time when something goes wrong with a song will take longer. If the band misses a cue or a singer is off key, the Song Leader has a difficult time shaking it off and moving on. They spent most of their time planning and prepping the songs so they want everything to go well and according to plan. When it does not, the train has been knocked off track and it will take some time to correct the derailment.

It takes a special leader to lead the congregation in song. The Song Leader understands that congregational song not only expresses a response to God, but also tells the story of God. Song Leaders must consider the voice of the congregation as utmost importance and give them the best chance to fulfill the biblical command of singing their praises to the Lord.

Worship Role: Song Leader

Worship Type: Corporate

Worship Gathering: Congregational; Family

Primary Responsibility: To lead the musical portions of a worship service

17

Worship Artist

Artistic creativity is not only God–given but one of the main ways whereby the power of God is unleashed, awakening both a thirst for justice and a hunger for beauty.

JOHN DE GRUCHY

A NUMBER OF YEARS ago I attended a very popular ministry conference held in Southern California. This conference was one high–energy, high–caliber presentation after another. From the popular speakers (both church and secular) to the music, lights and multi–media, every element was planned to pump up the audience. Even the announcements were done in spectacular fashion. The purpose of the conference was to get the attendees excited and encouraged about ministry.

As with any conference of this nature, the music was led by popular Worship Artists. Their performances were high–energy, complete with special effect lighting, creative videos, and even fog machines. The music was cranked up to eleven on the volume knob (on a scale of one to ten). The musicians were top–notch players that had evidently worked very hard to perfect their craft. Each of the artists had recordings for sale at the conference bookstore.

The Worship Artist's main focus is to lead people in personal worship and encourage them to live a lifestyle of worship. They record albums of worship songs as a way to encourage people in their daily personal worship times. They will also perform at conferences and put on concerts. Here, their focus continues to be personal worship, it just happens to be in a corporate setting. The Worship Artist will also encourage worshipers to worship God through all aspects of their lives. They desire for people to live in ways that bring glory to God and invite others into a relationship with the Lord.

When performing in corporate settings, the Worship Artist leads worship in a festival type gathering. Specialized lighting, videos, and fog machines often characterize the festival gathering. These times serve as an opportunity for the Worship Artist to encourage worshipers to continue to fight the good fight and trust in the Lord. The Worship Artist's ministry is a more performance–based ministry to build up the Body of Christ and encourage them on the journey.

In their actions of leading worship, the Worship Artist will often go where most people can't follow. What I mean is the artist is generally a superior musician and is able to play instruments and sing in ways that impress and awe the observer. Because the average person observing the performance is not as skilled of a musician, they are left behind. You'll often hear statements from observers like, "I wish I could play like that," or, "I wish I could sing like that." Comments like, "Wow, they tore the roof off!"

Yet, it's not solely about the musical talent. Many times, through the Worship Artist's skilled musicianship, the observer is moved to worship. It is when this happens that the Worship Artist fulfills their calling. The Worship Artist truly loves the Lord, loves to worship God and deeply desires for others to do the same. Rory Noland, director of Heart of the Artist Ministries, says, "The worshiping artist is someone who does his or her art as a deliberate act of worship to the Triune God."[1]

The Supreme Artist

I've said it before, but I believe it bears repeating: There is nothing wrong with being a Worship Artist. The character of a Worship Artist takes after the character of God. God the Father is the supreme Artist and the author of creation. One popular biblical metaphor for this is God as a potter.

> But now, O Lord, you are our Father; we are the clay, and you are our potter; we are all the work of your hand. (Isa 68:4)

We are God's work of art.

1. Rory Noland. "The Worshiping Artist." *Worship Leader* (July/August 2011) 29.

> For we are God's handiwork, created in Christ Jesus to do good works, which God prepared in advance for us to do. (Eph 2:10 NIV)

He is working on us as an artist works on a piece of art—as a potter works on clay.

Artistry and creativity begins and ends with God. In Genesis we read about the beginning: "In the beginning, God created the heavens and the earth. The earth was without form and void, and darkness was over the face of the deep. And the Spirit of God was hovering over the face of the waters" (Gen 1:1–2). And in Revelation we read about the end—and the new beginning: "Then I saw a new heaven and a new earth, for the first heaven and the first earth had passed away, and the sea was no more. And I saw the holy city, the new Jerusalem, coming down out of heaven from God, prepared as a bride adorned for her husband" (Rev 21:1–2).

As the ultimate Artist, God has created his children to be artistic. Bezalel is one such example:

> See, I have called by name Bezalel the son of Uri, son of Hur, of the tribe of Judah, and I have filled him with the Spirit of God, with ability and intelligence, with knowledge and all craftsmanship, to devise artistic designs, to work in gold, silver, and bronze, in cutting stones for setting, and in carving wood, to work in every craft. (Exod 31:2–5)

This biblical passage is significant as it connects ability, wisdom, and knowledge to artistry. It is also noteworthy that Bezalel was described as being "filled with the Spirit of God." In fact, the name Bezalel means "in the very shadow of God." He is not only the first artist depicted in the Bible, but the first person said to have been filled with the spirit of God.

Artistry is found throughout the pages of Scripture. While Bezalel can be considered the father of sacred art, Jubal (see Gen 4:21) could be considered the father of sacred music. Miriam (see Exod 15:20–21) and David (see 2 Sam 6:5, 14) danced before the Lord and Jesus himself was a carpenter and consummate storyteller. The design and construction of Solomon's temple and other various art forms reiterate that the Bible is filled with the creation and performance of an abundance of sacred art.

Excellence vs. Perfectionism

Some may say the actions of a Worship Artist are too performance driven, but there is nothing inherently wrong with performing our worship for God and encouraging others toward God in worship.[2] Conflicts arise however when Worship Artists are brought in to the church to *lead* Congregational Worship. In these instances, the congregation begins to feel as though the worship service is a "performance"—actions done for them rather than by them. This feeling of performance driven worship is a result of who is leading the service. A more appropriate setting for the Worship Artist is the Festival Worship Gathering, not the Congregational Worship Gathering.

God calls certain people to become Worship Artists. For those called to this particular role, their job is to fulfill that calling to the best of their ability. This means becoming excellent at their craft and displaying creativity in the implementation of that craft, while maintaining God as the center of all they do. Worship Artists must understand their calling and serve in appropriate settings.

As a result of focusing on pursuing excellence in their craft, the Worship Artist will oftentimes struggle with perfectionism.[3] They can easily maximize the negative and minimize the positive. As with the Song Leader, when something deviates from what was planned, or something goes wrong with the presentation, the Worship Artist may struggle to recover. Oftentimes the memory of the entire performance is swayed by that one mistake. Rory Noland shares his experience,

> Several years ago I did an arrangement of an old hymn for a Thanksgiving service. I treated it in a variety of styles, and it was supposed to be fun, celebratory, and worshipful. Well, there was one section that I counted off at a tempo that was too slow, and the band locked on to that tempo and I couldn't get them out of it. The arrangement

2. Barry Liesch provides an operational definition of performance in light of corporate worship: "To perform is . . . to do something complicated or difficult with skill in public with a view toward serving or ministering." (Liesch, *The New Worship*, 127). Since worship is an action, performance contains the dimension of *skill*, a word frequently used in the Old Testament. The New Testament counterpart to skill is *giftedness*. In the church, gifted people are capable of skilled work, integrated with and for the purpose of serving the entire congregation.

3. I mention the struggle of perfectionism here, not because the other worship leadership roles do not struggle with this issue, but because it seems that the Worship Artist may struggle with it more than the other roles. Regardless, every person called to worship leadership must guard against perfectionism.

played on at the wrong tempo. I don't know how long it actually was, but it felt like forever to me.... The rest of the service went very well, but I went home depressed because of that one short section (ironically, the hymn was "Count Your Blessings").[4]

Our culture has encouraged artists to seek technique to the level of avoiding errors at all costs. Artists are taught to seek perfection but call it pursuing excellence. Michael Bauer states,

> In contemporary society, perfection is often confused with excellence. From the standpoint of Christian anthropology, perfection is an ill-fated standard in this world because it does not reflect the reality of the human person, who is out of sync with God and yet ultimately destined for union with God.[5]

The confusion between excellence and perfectionism must be guarded at all times by Worship Artists. The temptation is to forget what we have been called to do and by whom we have been called. I remember being at a worship concert and the lead singer was having technical issues with his in-ear monitor and guitar. From the audience I could tell something was going on, but I continued to enjoy the music and turn my attention toward God. All of a sudden, the lead singer stopped singing, abruptly turned around, ripped the earpiece out of his ears, slammed his guitar onto the guitar stand and walked off stage. He didn't even finish the song. It was evident he was upset that there were technical issues. I remember thinking how sad that this person had turned the concert into being about the performance rather than pointing people to God. Worship Artists must remember their calling—to utilize their craft to worship the Lord and encourage others to do the same. It is not about being perfect in your performance, it is about offering your most excellent effort for the glory of God.

God is not seeking perfection. He does not desire perfect offerings, but wholehearted worship offered by imperfect people. This is not to say that artists should not be held, nor hold themselves, to a certain standard of excellence. We do not want to offer "cheap grace" where mistakes are ignored and mediocrity is championed. We must strive to offer God our most excellent offerings of worship, but not get so caught up in offering a perfect sacrifice that we miss the point of the offering in the first place. The

---

4. Noland, *The Heart of the Artist*, 124.

5. Bauer, *Arts Ministry*, 277.

goal for the Worship Artist is to offer God their most excellent offering as a way of worshiping him and encourage others in their worship of God.

Confusing the Roles

Problems arise when Worship Artists, and church leadership, confuse the role of the Worship Artist with that of the Worship Leader. The Worship Leader's job is not to perform worship for the congregation, but to encourage the congregation to perform their worship for the Lord. Therefore the congregation becomes the performers doing the work of worship. The Worship Artist, on the other hand, will perform their artistry in a way that will encourage others to worship the Lord through personal and lifestyle worship practices. Sometimes corporate worship will occur during the Festival Worship Gathering, but not always. The Worship Artist's primary responsibility is not to help the audience[6] perform their worship, but to perform themselves in such a way that the audience is encouraged to worship on their own.

Think about your favorite Worship Artist—someone you would pay money to see in concert. Imagine them leading worship during their concert. Now imagine many people in the audience not singing along, with arms crossed. It is very apparent that they are not engaged in worship. How will this affect the Worship Artist? Will this change what the Worship Artist is doing on the platform? I have seen this first-hand and the answer is no. The Worship Artist will continue to do their songs as rehearsed (or as recorded on their album). They will rarely deviate from their plan. Maybe they will work harder in an effort to engage the audience more, but not much. After the concert they may say something like, "That was a 'dead room.'" This is the exact opposite of a Worship Leader leading worship in a Congregational Gathering. If the congregation is clearly not engaging in worship on a Sunday morning, the Worship Leader must alter the plan in order to assist the congregation in their worship.

---

6. Notice I used the word audience rather than congregation. This is because a group of people observing a Worship Artist is an audience. They have come to see the Worship Artist implement their artistry in a way that is professional and excellent. The Worship Artist is generally a professional and can do things that the average person in the audience cannot do.

Confusing the Gatherings

Too often worshipers confuse the types of gatherings and turn the Congregational Gathering into a Worship Artist performance venue. Worship Artists primarily lead worship in festival type gatherings. Yet, worshipers often attend the festival gatherings, are attracted to the high–energy worship experience, and desire for the worship in their church services to imitate the worship experienced in the festival gathering. The same goes for those in church leadership. A Worship Artist may be fun and top-notch quality, but the Sunday morning congregational gathering is not the best place for a Worship Artist to use their gifts. The Worship Artist really doesn't have the intention of getting out of the way and helping the congregation perform their worship. During a worship concert (or Festival Worship Gathering) does the Worship Artist want the audience to worship God? Do they want the audience to be encouraged and blessed by the performance? Yes, absolutely! The Worship Artist, however, is primarily encouraging personal and lifestyle worship. The Sunday morning gathering is for corporate worship—a time to join with our brothers and sisters in the Lord, locking arms and raising voices, magnifying the Lord together for what he has done. The congregation becomes the performers of worship and God is the audience. In a Festival Worship Gathering the Worship Artist is the performer while the people, and God, are the audience.

Those in worship leadership must understand their calling and the difference in worship gatherings. The Worship Artist is not necessarily called to lead worship on Sunday mornings for a worship service. It is a different approach to leading and many times, Worship Artists struggle to incorporate the congregation, as is the primary purpose of the congregational worship gathering.

Let me take you back to the ministry conference mentioned at the beginning of this chapter. I remember one church leader in attendance at the conference with me, in the middle of one of the sessions, turned to me with stars in their eyes and said, "This is how our church's worship should be." This person confused the types of gatherings. We must remember that the conference and the church worship service are two different gatherings. Worship led by a Worship Artist should not necessarily be done in a church worship service that is designed for congregational worship led by a Worship Leader. These are two different worship gatherings and two different leadership callings. We must not confuse the two. To do so will invite frustration and disappointment into ministry.

Worship Role: Worship Artist

Worship Type: Personal; Lifestyle

Worship Gathering: Festival

Primary Responsibility: To build up the body of Christ and encourage them on their journey of worshiping God

18

Worship Pastor

In the land of the spirit, you cannot walk by the light of someone else's lamp.
You want to borrow mine. I'd rather teach you how to make your own.

ANTHONY DE MELLO
20TH CENTURY JESUIT

THE KEY WORD IN the title of this next worship leadership role is the word "pastor." The primary responsibility of the Worship Pastor is the care and spiritual formation of those in the worship ministries, as well as the congregation. The vital job of shepherding is a central responsibility for the Worship Pastor. Shepherding requires a leader to take on the role of a priest while being committed to the entire body of Christ.

A Priestly Role

The idea of the Worship Pastor taking on the role of priest comes to us from the Old Testament. Old Testament priests were not self-appointed, but were chosen by God with a specific purpose: to serve God with their lives by offering sacrifices. To be a priest was a high calling:

> Now this is what you shall do to them to consecrate them, that they may serve me as priests . . . You shall take the anointing oil and pour it on his head and anoint him. Then you shall bring his

sons and put coats on them, and you shall gird Aaron and his sons with sashes and bind caps on them. And the priesthood shall be theirs by a statute forever. Thus you shall ordain Aaron and his sons . . . I will consecrate the tent of meeting and the altar. Aaron also and his sons I will consecrate to serve me as priests. (Exod 29:1a, 7–9, 44)

The Lord said to Aaron, "You, your sons and your family are to bear the responsibility for offenses connected with the sanctuary, and you and your sons alone are to bear the responsibility for offenses connected with the priesthood. Bring your fellow Levites from your ancestral tribe to join you and assist you when you and your sons minister before the tent of the covenant law. They are to be responsible to you and are to perform all the duties of the tent, but they must not go near the furnishings of the sanctuary or the altar. Otherwise both they and you will die. They are to join you and be responsible for the care of the tent of meeting—all the work at the tent—and no one else may come near where you are.

You are to be responsible for the care of the sanctuary and the altar, so that my wrath will not fall on the Israelites again. I myself have selected your fellow Levites from among the Israelites as a gift to you, dedicated to the Lord to do the work at the tent of meeting. But only you and your sons may serve as priests in connection with everything at the altar and inside the curtain. I am giving you the service of the priesthood as a gift. Anyone else who comes near the sanctuary is to be put to death." (Num 18:1–7)

The responsibilities of the priesthood were specific. Not only that, they were intense. If not carried out meticulously, there were extreme consequences. This was a high and honored role. After all, the priests were to offer sacrifices for the people. They served as mediators between the people of God and God himself. What an awe–some privilege and incredible responsibility.

The role of the priest, as established by God, remained in tact for centuries. It is not until the New Testament, that we see an adjustment to the priesthood. Christ our High Priest became the once for all sacrifice for sin (Heb 10:12), and there is no more sacrifice for sin that need be made (Heb 10:26). As the priests once offered sacrifices in the temple, Peter makes it clear that God has chosen Christians . . .

. . . to be a holy priesthood, to offer spiritual sacrifices acceptable to God through Jesus Christ. . . . But you are a chosen race, a royal

priesthood, a holy nation, a people for his own possession, that
you may proclaim the excellencies of him who called you out of
darkness into his marvelous light. (1 Pet 2:5b, 9)

To be chosen by God to be a priest was a privilege and we see, according to
this passage, that all believers have been chosen by God. In the Old Testament tabernacle and temple, there were places where only the priests could
go. What's more, the most holy part of the tabernacle, called the Holy of
Holies, behind a thick veil, was a special place where only the high priest
could enter, and at that, only once a year on the Day of Atonement when
he made a sin offering on behalf of all the people. And yet, because of Jesus' death upon the cross of Calvary, the veil has been torn permitting all
believers direct access to the throne of God through Jesus Christ our great
High Priest (see Heb 4:14–16). What a privilege to be able to access the very
throne of God directly, not through any earthly priest.

> The priesthood of all believers . . . means that in the community
> of saints, God has constructed his body such that we are all priests
> to one another. Priesthood of all believers has more to do with
> the believer's service than with an individual's position or status.
> We are all believer–priests. We all stand equally before God. Such
> standing does not negate specific giftedness or calling. It rather
> enhances our giftedness as each one of us individually and col-
> lectively does his part to build the body (Eph 4:11–16). We are all
> priests. We are all responsible.[1]

While the priesthood of believers is an essential Christian doctrine, ac-
cepted by most Christians, there is also a priestly role that Pastors, and in our
case, Worship Pastors, must assume. This role must not be exercised from
a position of superiority because all in the body of Christ are equal.[2] Yet a
chain of command is not only biblical but also essential for people living in
community with one another. David's shepherding of Israel illustrates how
God uses "under–shepherds" to oversee his followers. The writer of the book
of Hebrews presents a model that points all the way back to Aaron:

> For every high priest taken from among men is appointed on behalf
> of men in things pertaining to God, in order to offer both gifts and
> sacrifices for sins; he can deal gently with the ignorant and misguid-
> ed, since he himself also is beset with weakness; and because of it he
> is obligated to offer sacrifices for sins, as for the people, so also for

1. Akin, *Perspectives on Church Government*, 37.
2. Altizer, *The Making of A Worship Leader*, 63.

himself. And no one takes the honor to himself, but receives it when he is called by God, even as Aaron was. (Heb 5:1–4)

Committed to the Body of Christ

The Worship Pastor must be fully committed to the body of Christ when serving God and his people. As we have seen earlier, the body of Christ is made up of people from various cultures, ethnicities and ages. Just as Jesus prayed for the unity of all believers (John 17:20–21), leaders should strive for unity among the congregation. The issue is that many people confuse unity with sameness. Being unified does not mean being the same or liking the same things. Instead, the Church is called to unity in the midst of diversity.

The Worship Pastor is concerned with providing an environment for the body of Christ to be formed spiritually. In the midst of our worship, we are being drawn closer to God. So, to lead worship means to teach theology. We should know more about God because of our worship. This is an important consideration for those that plan worship services. As we lead in worship we are putting words and thoughts on the lips and hearts of the congregation. John Witvliet states,

> As worship leaders, we have the important and terrifying task of placing words of prayer on people's lips. It happens every time we choose a song and write a prayer. We also have the holy task of being stewards of God's Word. Our choices of which scripture readings and themes will be featured in worship represent a degree of control over people's spiritual diets, how they feed on the bread of life, the Word of God. For holy tasks like these, the church needs more than craftspeople, coordinators, and performers. . . . The church needs pastoral people to plan and lead worship.[3]

So the question to ask is: Am I thinking pastorally about the worship elements I am selecting for the church?

The Pastoral Musician

Every part of the church's worship should be looked at through a pastoral lens. Allow me to take a moment to focus on the musical aspects of a worship service. This is one area that I believe is in desperate need of help in

3. Witvliet, *Worship Seeking Understanding*, 282.

our churches. Are we thinking pastorally about the music selection in our worship services? This is a critical question to ask as a pastoral musician thinks about music in a special way. Constance Cherry states, "A pastoral musician is a leader with developed skill and God-given responsibility for selecting and employing music in worship that will serve the actions of the liturgy, while reflecting on theological, contextual, and cultural considerations, all for the ultimate purpose of glorifying God."[4] In her excellent book on worship planning, Cherry gives the following list of considerations for the pastoral musician:[5]

- They embrace and live the Christian faith.
- They have a developing spiritual maturity.
- They have a sense of vocational call to worship ministry.
- They have primary responsibilities in music and worship ministry.
- They understand the relationship between music and liturgy.
- They understand that music is a servant to the text.
- They are accountable to God and to others for excellence.
- They view his/her duties holistically, with sensitivity to the larger purposes of worship, the Christian Year, orthodox praxis, etc.
- They understand the community of faith and the special nature of music's role within that community.
- They select and employ music not for music's sake, but for a greater purpose.
- They consider the Christian community and its need to proclaim the truth and respond to the truth through music.
- They are not primarily interested in music which is passively received, but in music which engages all worshipers.
- They seek to move worshipers from the role of audience to the role of active participants.
- They are interested in breadth of song—not only stylistically, but also in tone.

4. Cherry, *The Worship Architect*, 180.

5. Ibid., 180.

- They understand that the gospel invites a variety of emotions, from gladness to sorrow, from that which comforts to that which convicts.

- They are theologically discriminating.

- They help the worshiping community to sing the whole story of God, from creation to eschaton.

The pastoral musician understands that the music portions of the service work together with the other worship elements of a service to provide the congregation with an opportunity to rehearse the story of God and respond to the ways in which he has revealed himself. At the forefront of the pastoral musician's mind is the question, "How are the worshipers being formed spiritually through the elements of worship in the service?" This question is the heartbeat of the Worship Pastor.

Although we think of Sunday as the primary day for pastoral ministry, many of the main responsibilities of the Worship Pastor may not even occur on a Sunday. As a Worship Pastor myself, much of my ministry occurs outside of the Sunday morning worship services. A Worship Pastor seeks opportunities to care, counsel and pray for the people that God has entrusted to them. This may occur midweek when the team gathers to pray for one another at rehearsal. It may occur in hospital rooms, at memorial services, at weddings, and a variety of other possibilities.

A Worship Pastor is generally ordained by a denomination or licensed for ministry by the church. This privilege allows the Worship Pastor to officiate for weddings, memorial services, and other formal functions as a way to care for the congregation and community.

Overall, the main function of a Worship Pastor is to train, mentor and equip the people of God for ministry all the while caring for and shepherding the flock. They hold the qualifications of an elder. Therefore, in addition to leading the congregation in elements of worship within a worship service, they also fulfill pastoral duties such as counseling, hospital visitations and congregational care.

Let me conclude this chapter with the words of John Witvliet:

> What the church needs most is not another hymnal, a new sound system, a revised prayer book, or another set of published scripts. What the church needs most are discerning, prayerful, joyous people who treat their work as worship planners and leaders as a holy, pastoral calling.[6]

6. Witvliet, *Worship Seeking Understanding*, 284.

Worship Role: Worship Pastor

Worship Type: Personal; Corporate; Lifestyle

Worship Gathering: Private; Family; Congregational; Festival

Primary Responsibility: To train, mentor, and equip the people of God while caring for and shepherding the congregation

Conclusion

Prayer and praise are the oars by which a man may row
his boat into the deep waters of the knowledge of Christ.

CHARLES H. SPURGEON

2 CHRONICLES TWENTY-FIVE TELLS us of a King named Amaziah who reigned over Jerusalem for twenty-nine years. He was a good king and did what was right in God's sight. But here's the kicker . . . he did not do it with all of his heart; "he did what was right in the eyes of the Lord, but not wholeheartedly" (2 Chr 25:2). You see, Amaziah obeyed God . . . most of the time. He worshiped God . . . somewhat. He dedicated his life to serving God . . . until something better came along. He sang all the right songs, he said all the right words, but he did not do it wholeheartedly.

Conversely, the Bible tells us of a man named Caleb who was one of two men, Joshua being the other, that was bold enough to stand up against ten men and trust the Lord's leading into the Promised Land. What jumps out at me most about Caleb is how Scripture describes him. Caleb is the only Old Testament character that the Bible repeatedly says followed the Lord fully and wholeheartedly (see Num 14:24, 32:12; Deut 1:36; Josh 14:8, 9, 14).

When you worship, are you like Amaziah or are you more like Caleb? Do you worship with all your heart? Do you give all of yourself as you respond to who God is and what he has done for you? When we see God for Who he is, we should see ourselves for who we are. When Isaiah saw God seated on the throne, he cried out, "Woe is me! For I am lost; for I am a man of unclean lips, and I dwell in the midst of a people of unclean lips;

for my eyes have seen the King, the Lord of hosts" (Isa 6:5). Annie Dillard in her essay "Expedition to the Pole" asks,

> Why do people in church seem like cheerful, brainless tourists on a packaged tour of the Absolute? . . . Does anyone have the foggiest idea what sort of power we blithely invoke? Or, as I suspect, does no one believe a word of it? The churches are children playing on the floor with their chemistry sets, mixing up a batch of TNT to kill a Sunday morning. It is madness to wear ladies' straw hats and velvet hats to church; we should all be wearing crash helmets. Ushers should issue life preservers and signal flares; they should lash us to our pews. For the sleeping god may wake someday and take offense, or the waking god may draw us to where we can never return.[1]

When God reveals himself, we can do nothing else but worship. When you worship, do you put aside all else and focus on Almighty God, your Lord and Savior? Do you do Mark 12:30: "Love the Lord your God with all your heart and with all your soul and with all your mind and with all your strength"? Not with some of your heart, but all of it. Puritan Stephen Charnock states,

> Without the heart it is not worship; it is a stage play; an acting a part without being that person really . . . a hypocrite. We may truly be said to worship God—though we want [lack] perfection; but we cannot be said to worship Him if we want [lack] sincerity. . . . As with a lutinist [musician] it is absurd to play one tune and sing another, so it is a foul thing to tell God one thing with our lips, and think another with our hearts.[2]

Asaph was one of the worship leaders assigned by King David to lead the people of Israel in worship. There are twelve Psalms attributed to Asaph. Notice the wholehearted worship found in his Psalm 77:

> I will remember the deeds of the Lord; yes, I will remember your wonders of old. I will ponder all your work, and meditate on your mighty deeds. Your way, O God, is holy. What god is great like our God? You are the God who works wonders; you have made known your might among the peoples. (Ps 77:11–14)

The quest we have taken through this book provided us with the answers to questions regarding the foundations of worship. We examined the

1. Dillard, *Teaching A Stone to Talk*, 40–41.
2. Charnock, *Discourses*, 225, 263.

three avenues of personal, corporate, and lifestyle worship that every Christian should practice. We considered four types of worship gatherings and the purpose of each gathering. And we were introduced to four worship leadership roles and the specific calling that accompanies each role. I pray our exploration has led to a greater understanding of how to worship God and fulfill the calling God has for our lives to lead others in worshiping him.

As we worship God Most High, let's follow Asaph's lead and commit to worshiping in awe and reverence. Let all else fade away and focus on the One who is all else.

A Word To Senior Pastors and Church Leadership

ONE OF THE GREATEST joys in ministry is being able to release a member of the body of Christ to minister in ways in which God has called them. As church leaders, it is our responsibility to train, mentor and equip the body to serve according to their passion and call. The same is true for those called to vocational ministry. Although serving in the church is a career for those called to vocational ministry, members of the body of Christ are also to fulfill the calling placed on their lives by God.

It is important to consider a person's calling and fitness when inviting them to lead the congregation in worship. There is no greater joy for a person called to a worship leadership role than to find the "right fit" at a church or ministry organization. There is a saying, "When you love what you do you'll never work a day in your life." There is deep satisfaction and a sense of fulfillment when you are obeying the Lord by following his call on your life in the right place. On the flip side, there is no greater frustration than for a person to be serving in the wrong role with unrealistic expectations placed upon them. When this occurs, it begins to feel every bit like a job without much satisfaction, joy or fulfillment.

My hope is that the material in this book has been helpful; not only for those serving in worship leadership roles, but also for those in church leadership making the decisions on polity and church structure.

The greatest way to support your worship leader is to create clear expectations and communicate them on a regular basis. Commit regular times to sit down with your worship leader and discuss the worship philosophy of the church and the expectations placed upon them. Be sure to use this time to encourage your worship leader. They have one of the most critical jobs in the church as they assist the congregation in their time of meeting with God. As you well know, this is not always an easy task. It should never be taken lightly and they need much encouragement and support along the way.

Before hiring a worship leader, prayerfully consider the roles of worship leadership found in this book: Worship Leader, Song Leader, Worship Artist and Worship Pastor. Which role does your church want? Better yet, which role does your church *need*? Some churches are able to hire multiple roles to create a worship leadership team. A Worship Pastor oversees the entire worship ministry and primarily cares for the spiritual welfare of those in the ministry, as well as the congregation. The Worship Leader leads worship in the church services or a Song Leader leads the musical portions of the service while other worship leaders (Worship Pastor, Elder, Associate Pastor, Senior Pastor) lead the congregation in the prayers, Scripture readings and other elements of worship. Whatever the case may be in your church, my prayer is that you (and your church) will see the differences in roles and prayerfully consider which would be the best fit for your church.

Pastor, a clear understanding of the worship leadership roles on your part will make for a smooth working relationship with the worship leader. Once you know which role you and your church needs, you can then communicate this with potential worship leaders. If your church needs someone to simply lead the musical portions of the service, but not the prayers, Scripture reading, etc. communicate that to the worship leader before you hire them. This will save a lot of head—and heart—ache in the future. If you are interviewing someone called by God to be a Worship Leader, than your expectation for them to be a Song Leader will be frustrating, for both you and them. The same goes for every worship leadership role. If you want a Worship Leader to lead not just the songs but also the "in-between" worship elements, those times of worship found in between the songs, be sure to hire someone called to the role of Worship Leader. This person will have a heart for thinking through and preparing prayers, they will be creative with how to present Scripture readings (responsively, congregationally, etc.), and they will value each element of worship as just as important as music. If you want a Worship Pastor, be sure to hire someone who has a deep passion for caring for the congregation beyond music and the arts. This person should have counseling skills and a listening ear. They should be concerned primarily with the spiritual health of the congregation, not whether the praise band has the best quality in-ear monitors.

One word of caution: many churches over the past couple of decades have hired Worship Artists to lead congregational worship. This is a mistake. As seen in chapter 17, the Worship Artist is primarily concerned with personal and lifestyle worship. The Sunday morning gathering is a congregational worship gathering focused on corporate worship. The congregation does not need an artist to perform worship for them. They need a Worship Leader who will lead them in their worship. I believe placing a Worship Artist in the role of leading the congregation at a Sunday morning worship service, in place of a Worship Leader, is a perfect example of a worship leadership role in the wrong worship gathering.

Pastor, I guess I can sum this up by saying, be proactive rather than reactive. When deciding upon a worship leader for your church, ask specific questions to find out about their passion and call to ministry. If the main passions of the worship leader is to record worship CDs, perform music at a level that attracts new visitors to the church, and provide outreach concerts on Friday nights, you probably have a Worship Artist on your hands and not really what the congregation needs for Sunday morning worship. This is a difficult path to walk and one that requires much discernment. You are in my prayers.

Selected Sources

Allen, Ronald and Gordon Borror. *Worship: Rediscovering the Missing Jewel.* Portland: Multnomah Press, 1982.

Altizer, Jim. *The Making of A Worship Leader.* Thousand Oaks: Sound & Light, 2011.

Bateman, Herbert W. IV. *Authentic Worship: Hearing Scripture's Voice, Applying Its Truths.* Grand Rapids: Kregel, 2002.

Bauer, Michael J. *Arts Ministry: Nurturing the Creative Life of God's People.* Grand Rapids: Wm. B. Eerdmans, 2013.

Best, Harold M. *Unceasing Worship: Biblical Perspectives on Worship and the Arts.* Downers Grove: InterVarsity Press, 2003.

Billheimer, Paul E. *Destined for the Throne: How Spiritual Warfare Prepares the Bride of Christ for Her Eternal Destiny.* Fort Washington: Christian Literature Crusade, 1975.

Brand, Chad Owen and R. Stanton Norman, eds. *Perspectives on Church Government: Five Views of Church Polity.* Nashville: B&H, 2004.

Chapell, Bryan. *Christ-Centered Worship: Letting the Gospel Shape Our Practice.* Grand Rapids: Baker Academic, 2009.

Cherry, Constance, Bounds and Brown. *Selecting Worship Songs: A Guide for Leaders.* Marion: Triangle, 2011.

Cherry, Constance. *The Worship Architect: A Blueprint for Designing Culturally Relevant and Biblically Faithful Services.* Grand Rapids: Baker Academic, 2010.

Clark, Paul B. Jr. *Tune My Heart to Sing Thy Grace: Worship Renewal Through Congregational Singing.* Bloomington: CrossBooks, 2010.

Dawn, Marva. *A Royal "Waste" Of Time: The Splendor of Worshiping God and Being Church for the World.* Grand Rapids: Wm. B. Eerdmans, 1999.

Dillard, Annie. *Teaching A Stone to Talk: Expeditions and Encounters.* London: Harper Perennial, 1984.

Furr, Gary and Milburn Price. *The Dialogue of Worship: Creating Space for Revelation and Response.* Macon: Smyth and Helwys, 1999.

Grudem, Wayne. *Systematic Theology: An Introduction to Biblical Doctrine.* Grand Rapids: Zondervan, 1994.

Hall, Thelma. *Too Deep for Words: Rediscovering Lectio Divina.* Mahwah: Paulist Press, 1988.

Hustad, Donald P. *Jubilate II: Church Music in Worship and Renewal.* Carol Stream: Hope, 1993.

Kenoly, Ron and Dick Bernal. *Lifting Him Up: How You Can Enter Into Spirit-Led Praise and Worship*. Orlando: Creation House, 1995.

Kidd, Reggie M. *With One Voice: Discovering Christ's Song In Our Worship*. Grand Rapids: Baker Books, 2005.

Kraeuter, Tom. *Developing an Effective Worship Ministry*. Lynnwood: Emerald Books, 1993.

———. *Worship Is ... What?: Re-Thinking Our Ideas About Worship*. Lynnwood: Emerald Books, 1996.

Labberton, Mark. *The Dangerous Act of Worship: Living God's Call to Justice*. Downers Grove: InterVarsity Press, 2007.

Lewis, C.S. *God In the Dock*. Grand Rapids: Wm. B. Eerdmans, 1970.

Liesch, Barry. *People In the Presence of God: Models and Directions for Worship*. Grand Rapids: Zondervan, 1988.

———. *The New Worship: Straight Talk on Music and the Church*. Grand Rapids: Baker Books, 1996.

Mulholland, M. Robert. *The Deeper Journey: The Spirituality of Discovering*. Downers Grove: InterVarsity Press, 2006.

Noland, Rory. *The Heart of the Artist: A Character-Building Guide for You and Your Ministry Team*. Grand Rapids: Zondervan, 1999.

———. *The Worshiping Artist: Equipping You and Your Ministry Team to Lead Others in Worship*. Grand Rapids: Zondervan, 2007.

Nouwen, Henri J.M. *In the Name of Jesus: Reflections on Christian Leadership*. New York: The Crossroad, 1989.

———. *The Way of the Heart: Connecting With God Through Prayer, Wisdom, and Silence*. New York: First Ballantine Books, 1983.

———. *With Burning Hearts: A Meditation on the Eucharistic Life*. Maryknoll: Orbis Books, 1994.

Old, Hughes Oliphant. *Leading in Prayer: A Workbook for Worship*. Grand Rapids: Wm. B. Eerdmans, 1995.

Parry, Robin. *Worshipping Trinity: Coming Back to the Heart of Worship*. Waynesboro: Paternoster, 2005.

Piper, John. *Let the Nations Be Glad: The Supremacy of God in Missions*. Grand Rapids: Baker Academic, 1993.

Read, Ken E. *Created to Worship: A Practical Guide to Leading the Christian Assembly*. Joplin: College Press, 2002.

Schaper, Robert. *In His Presence: Appreciating Your Worship Tradition*. Nashville: Thomas Nelson, 1984.

Torrance, James B. *Worship, Community and the Triune God of Grace*. Downer's Grove: InterVarsity Press, 1996.

Tozer, A.W. *The Pursuit of God*. Harrisburg: Christian Publications, 1948.

———. *Whatever Happened To Worship?* Camp Hill: Christian Publications, 1985.

Webber, Robert E. *Ancient-Future Time: Forming Spirituality through the Christian Year*. Grand Rapids: Baker Books, 2004.

———. *Ancient-Future Worship: Proclaiming and Enacting God's Narrative*. Grand Rapids: Baker Books, 2008.

———. *Journey to Jesus: The Worship, Evangelism, and Nurture Mission of the Church*. Nashville: Abingdon, 2001.

———. *Worship Old and New*. Grand Rapids: Zondervan, 1982.

Willard, Dallas and Jan Johnson. *Renovation of the Heart in Daily Practice: Experiments in Spiritual Transformation.* Colorado Springs: NavPress, 2006.

Willimon, William. *The Service of God: How Worship and Ethics are Related.* Nashville: Abingdon Press, 1983.

Witvliet, John. *Worship Seeking Understanding: Windows Into Christian Practice.* Grand Rapids: Baker Academic, 2003.

Wren, Brian. *Praying Twice: The Music and Words of Congregational Song.* Louisville: Westminster John Knox Press, 2000.

Recommended Resources

Websites/Blogs/Music

Worship Quest Ministries

Worship Quest Ministries is designed to encourage and enhance worship renewal within the church. You will find resources for and information on congregational worship.

www.worshipquestministries.com

Roadmaps For Worship

Dr. Jim Altizer has developed a website providing educational and practical resources for worship leaders.

www.roadmapsforworship.com

Walt Harrah

Worship scripts and music resources for congregational worship.

www.waltharrah.com

Keith and Kristyn Getty

Music and resources from modern hymn writers Keith and Kristyn Getty.

www.gettymusic.com

Worship Better

How do you select songs for the congregation at your church to sing? Is it based on the key of the song, popularity, or radio play? Worship Better assists you in selecting songs based on theological, musical, and lyrical considerations.

www.worshipbetter.com

Hymnary

A comprehensive resource for hymns and hymn tunes; includes hymns from over 5,000 hymnals.

www.hymnary.org

The Worship Community

The forums on this site can be particularly helpful.

www.theworshipcommunity.com

Weekly Scripture

An online resource with Scripture readings, prayers, and a variety of other resources based on the lectionary.

www.textweek.com

Worship Education

Calvin Institute for Christian Worship

Directed by John Witvliet, the Calvin Institute for Christian Worship offers a great annual worship symposium (conference). Their website offers a multitude of resources.

www.worship.calvin.edu

The Robert E. Webber Institute for Worship Studies

The Robert E. Webber Institute for Worship Studies exists to form servant leaders in Christian worship renewal and education through graduate academic praxis, grounded in biblical, historical, theological, cultural and missiological reflection in community.

www.iws.edu

Ten Worship Books You Should Have On Your Shelf

The Making Of A Worship Leader by Jim Altizer

Unceasing Worship: Biblical Perspectives on Worship and the Arts by Harold Best

Christ-Centered Worship: Letting the Gospel Shape Our Practice by Bryan Chapell

The Worship Architect: A Blueprint for Designing Culturally and Biblically Faithful Services by Constance Cherry

A Royal "Waste" of Time: The Splendor of Worshiping God and Being Church for the World by Marva Dawn

Engaging With God: A Biblical Theology of Worship by David Peterson

Recalling the Hope of Glory: Biblical Worship from the Garden to the New Creation by Allen P. Ross

Whatever Happened to Worship?: A Call to True Worship By A.W. Tozer

Ancient-Future Worship: Proclaiming and Enacting God's Narrative by Robert E. Webber

Renovation of the Heart: Putting on the Character of Christ by Dallas Willard

Other Noteworthy Resources

The Book of Daily Prayer

Compiled by Robert Webber

The Book of Daily Prayer offers a convenient guide to prayer on a day-to-day basis throughout the year encouraging a lifestyle of worship based prayer that is consistent and fruitful.

The Worship Sourcebook

The Worship Sourcebook is one of the most substantial resources available for traditional and contemporary church worship services. Filled with beautifully prepared prayers, stirring liturgies, and useful service plans, The Worship Sourcebook is an essential tool for any church looking to freshen up its resources without changing its worship style.

For more information, see http://www.re-formedworship.org/article/march-2004/well-chosen-words-introducing-worship-sourcebook.

(See additional suggestions in the Selected Sources section)

APPENDIX 1

Definitions of Worship

Worship is an active response to God whereby we declare his worth
—RONALD ALLEN

Worship is the human response to the self-revelation of the triune God
—ROBERT BATEMAN

Worship is acknowledging that someone or something else is greater—worth more—and by consequence, to be obeyed, feared, and adored . . . Worship is the sign that in giving myself completely to someone or something, I want to be mastered by it
—HAROLD BEST

Worship is reverential human acts of submission and homage before the divine Sovereign, in response to his gracious revelation of himself, and in accordance with his will
—DANIEL BLOCK

Worship is a God–initiated, God–sanctioned, gifted response to his divine revelation
—MATT BOSWELL

[Worship] is to acknowledge Him to be, as He is, the only source of all virtue, justice, holiness, wisdom, truth, power, goodness, mercy, life, and salvation
—JOHN CALVIN

Worship is the proper response of all moral, sentient beings to God, ascribing all honor and worth to their Creator–God precisely because he is worthy, delightfully so
—D. A. CARSON

Worship is giving God the best that He has given you
—OSWALD CHAMBERS

Worship is the adoring response of the creature to the infinite majesty of God
—ROBERT E. COLEMAN

Christian worship is the response of men to the Divine call, to the 'mighty deeds' of God, culminating in the redemptive act of Christ
—GEORGE FLOROVSKY

Worship is our response to the overtures of love from the heart of the Father
—RICHARD FOSTER

Worship is our response, both personal and corporate, to God for who He is, and what He has done; expressed in and by the things we say and the way we live
—LOUIE GIGLIO

Worship is a full confrontation with the self–revealed God of the Scriptures with ample opportunity to respond. Worship is any and every worthy response to God
—DONALD HUSTAD

Christian worship is the response of God's redeemed people to His self-revelation that exalts God's glory in Christ in our minds, affections, and wills, in the power of the Holy Spirit
—BOB KAUFLIN

Worship is God's enjoyment of us and our enjoyment of him. Worship is a response to the father/child relationship
—GRAHAM KENDRICK

Worship is wholehearted, passionate adoration of our Creator/Redeemer
—TOM KRAEUTER

Worship is the act of declaring to God his worth, affirming who he is and what he has done, and responding to him in praise, adoration, thanksgiving and awe
—BARRY LIESCH

Worship is the dramatic celebration of God in his supreme worth in such a manner that his "worthiness" becomes the norm and inspiration of human living
—RALPH P. MARTIN

Worship is our response to the presence of God
—RORY NOLAND

Worship is the response of an adoring heart to the magnificence of God. In the highest sense of the word, it is the occupation of the created with the Creator Himself. It is the pure joy of magnifying the One whose name is above every other name
—RON OWENS

Worship of the living and true God is essentially an engagement with him on the terms that he proposes and in the way that he alone makes possible
—DAVID PETERSON

Worship is our soul bowing before God in adoring contemplation of Him
—ARTHUR PINK

Worship is the activity of the new life of a believer in which, recognizing the fullness of the Godhead as it is revealed in the person of Jesus Christ and His mighty redemptive acts, he seeks by the power of the Holy Spirit to render to the living God the glory, honor, and submission which are His due
—ROBERT RAYBURN

Worship is the expression of a relationship in which God the Father reveals himself and his love in Christ, and by His Holy Spirit administers grace to which we respond in faith, gratitude and obedience
—ROBERT SCHAPER

To worship is to quicken the conscience by the holiness of God, to feed the mind with the truth of God, to purge the imagination by the beauty of God, to open the heart to the love of God, to devote the will to the purpose of God
—WILLIAM TEMPLE

Worship is the total adoring response of man to the one eternal God self revealed in time
—EVELYN UNDERHILL

Worship is a personal meeting with God in which we honor, magnify and glorify him for his person and actions
—ROBERT E. WEBBER

Worship is the believer's response to all they are – mind, emotions, will, body—to what God is and says and does
—WARREN WIERSBE

APPENDIX 2

The Athanasian Creed

Whosoever will be saved, before all things it is necessary that he hold the catholic faith. Which faith except every one do keep whole and undefiled; without doubt he shall perish everlastingly.

And the catholic faith is this: That we worship one God in Trinity, and Trinity in Unity; Neither confounding the Persons; nor dividing the Essence. For there is one Person of the Father; another of the Son; and another of the Holy Ghost. But the Godhead of the Father, of the Son, and of the Holy Ghost, is all one; the Glory equal, the Majesty coeternal. Such as the Father is; such is the Son; and such is the Holy Ghost.

The Father uncreated; the Son uncreated; and the Holy Ghost uncreated. The Father unlimited; the Son unlimited; and the Holy Ghost unlimited. The Father eternal; the Son eternal; and the Holy Ghost eternal.

And yet they are not three eternals; but one eternal. As also there are not three uncreated; nor three infinites, but one uncreated; and one infinite.

So likewise the Father is Almighty; the Son Almighty; and the Holy Ghost Almighty. And yet they are not three Almighties; but one Almighty.

So the Father is God; the Son is God; and the Holy Ghost is God. And yet they are not three Gods; but one God. So likewise the Father is Lord; the Son Lord; and the Holy Ghost Lord. And yet not three Lords; but one Lord.

For like as we are compelled by the Christian verity; to acknowledge every Person by himself to be God and Lord; So are we forbidden by the catholic religion; to say, There are three Gods, or three Lords. The Father is made of none; neither created, nor begotten. The Son is of the Father alone; not made, nor created; but begotten. The Holy Ghost is of the Father and of the Son; neither made, nor created, nor begotten; but proceeding.

So there is one Father, not three Fathers; one Son, not three Sons; one Holy Ghost, not three Holy Ghosts. And in this Trinity none is before, or after another; none is greater, or less than another. But the whole three Persons are coeternal, and coequal. So that in all things, as aforesaid; the Unity in Trinity, and the Trinity in Unity, is to be worshipped. He therefore that will be saved, let him thus think of the Trinity.

Furthermore it is necessary to everlasting salvation; that he also believe faithfully the Incarnation of our Lord Jesus Christ. For the right Faith is, that we believe and confess; that our Lord Jesus Christ, the Son of God, is God and Man; God, of the Essence of the Father; begotten before the worlds; and Man, of the Essence of his Mother, born in the world. Perfect God; and perfect Man, of a reasonable soul and human flesh subsisting.

Equal to the Father, as touching his Godhead; and inferior to the Father as touching his Manhood. Who although he is God and Man; yet he is not two, but one Christ. One; not by conversion of the Godhead into flesh; but by assumption of the Manhood by God. One altogether; not by confusion of Essence; but by unity of Person. For as the reasonable soul and flesh is one man; so God and Man is one Christ; Who suffered for our salvation; descended into hell; rose again the third day from the dead. He ascended into heaven, he sitteth on the right hand of the God the Father Almighty, from whence he will come to judge the quick and the dead. At whose coming all men will rise again with their bodies; And shall give account for their own works. And they that have done good shall go into life everlasting; and they that have done evil, into everlasting fire.

This is the catholic faith; which except a man believe truly and firmly, he cannot be saved.

APPENDIX 3

Convergence Worship :: Old, New, Borrowed, Blue

Convergence worship is celebrating God in a manner reflective of local traditions expressed in ways relevant to the contemporary worshiper.

THERE ARE MANY DETAILS that need to be considered when planning a wedding. I realize that I only grasp a small portion of wedding preparation because, after all, I am a guy and my wife did the majority of the planning and prep work for our wedding (whatever you do, don't ask her about the day before our wedding when I went to the beach with my groomsmen while she sat at her parents' house tying bows on all of the wedding programs). There is a tradition that is common when it comes to weddings. This tradition stems from an old English rhyme "Something olde, something new, something borrowed, something blue, and a silver sixpence in your shoe." As a token of love, family members and the bride's attendants gave old, new, borrowed, and blue items as well as a sixpence to the bride on her wedding day. Brides are still working the old, new, borrowed, and blue objects into their weddings today.

When I think of convergence worship, I think it is important for worship planners to follow the lead of this wedding tradition and incorporate each part of the phrase into the worship experience. Let's take a look at convergence worship in light of the phrase.

Something Old

This does not mean to incorporate worship elements that are outdated. The term "old" refers to those elements of worship that have longevity. We are not the first ones on this journey of worship. There are many who have gone before and have provided wonderful examples of how to worship the Lord. Let's lean on them instead of ignoring or devaluing them.

- Music: Songs that have stood the test of time and countless theologians. These include traditional hymns, older praise choruses, and classical works.

- Art: Fine and performance art from historical periods other than the here and now.

- Prayers and quotes from ancient Church Fathers and those theologians that have come before.

Something New

It is also important to incorporate new elements of worship. God did not stop his work with the New Testament apostles. He continues to work today. Incorporating elements of worship by and from current Christians is beneficial to the church.

- Music: Sing songs that are currently being created. These include modern hymns and current praise choruses; as well as new arrangements of older songs. When Scripture calls us to "sing to the Lord a new song," (Psalm 96:1, et al) I don't believe it simply means songs written today. It also means new arrangements, versions, and interpretations of existing songs. Worship Artists have been doing this for a while now—taking an older hymn and creating a new version in order to breathe new life into the beloved hymns of the past. This has resulted in a rediscovery of texts and tunes by a new generation of worshipers. Singing a new song to the Lord can mean singing an older song in a new way.

- Art: Utilize various art forms from current artists, including (and especially) those within your congregation.

CONVERGENCE WORSHIP :: OLD, NEW, BORROWED, BLUE

- Prayers and quotes from modern day theologians, including your own pastor: use a quote from a previous sermon to reiterate a point and encourage your congregation.

Something Borrowed

Worship planners should incorporate worship elements from other cultures and ethnicities, denominations and traditions. Here, diversity is the key.

- Music: Global music; singing songs from cultures different than our own help us connect with the broader body of Christ.
- Art: Fine and performance art from cultures other than your own.
- Prayers and quotes from theologians of a different tradition.
    * being careful to consider theological and doctrinal differences

Something Blue

Our worship should be a celebration of Christ. In order to celebrate well, we must be able to lament well. We are not used to worshiping when all is not right with the world. Moreover, I would say we don't know *how* to worship well when things are not going smoothly in our lives. Yet ministry, and worship leading, deals with real life. And real life is messy. What is done in these situations has the potential to preach the gospel more than a year's worth of sermons.

If we use the Psalms as a guideline, we see they are filled with praise, but also lament.

> How long, O Lord? Will you forget me forever?
> How long will you hide your face from me?
> How long must I take counsel in my soul
> and have sorrow in my heart all the day?
> How long shall my enemy be exalted over me?
> Consider and answer me, O Lord my God;
> light up my eyes, lest I sleep the sleep of death,
> lest my enemy say, "I have prevailed over him,"
> lest my foes rejoice because I am shaken.
> But I have trusted in your steadfast love;
> my heart shall rejoice in your salvation.

I will sing to the Lord,
because he has dealt bountifully with me. (Psalm 13)

It is natural and appropriate to lament. The early church included confession as part of their worship on a regular basis. Today, confession is not regularly used, but I believe should be brought back to regular occurrence. In today's contemporary church, we gather together and jump right into praising God. Does this mean we have already confessed the sins we committed during the week? Or, that we did not sin at all that week, or that morning on the way to worship? Confession of sin, and lament, is an appropriate, and I believe vital aspect of our worship.

As defined earlier, convergence worship is celebrating God in a manner reflective of local traditions expressed in ways relevant to the contemporary worshiper. When planning convergence worship, be sure to incorporate elements that are old, new, borrowed and blue.

APPENDIX 4

How to Practice *Lectio Divina*

1. Read and Listen to a Text (*Lectio*)

Choose a text of Scripture to read slowly. *Listen* to the text with your heart and mind. *Hear* the Lord speaking to you in the text. Allow yourself to simply *be* with the text in an open and vulnerable way.

2. Reflect on the Word (*Meditatio*)

By faith assume this text is *addressed to you*. Because God has "translated himself into our humanity, in Jesus," Jesus truly speaks to us by the spirit in a language we can understand. At the *meditatio* level it is important to ask, "What is it that you want me to hear?"

3. Let the Word Touch Your Heart (Prayer, *Oratio*)

In *Oratio*, the word of God goes deeper into the self and becomes "the prayer of the heart." In this prayer open your heart so that his light may enter. The goal is like that of St. Augustine, who cried, "O God, our hearts are made for thee, and they shall be restless until they rest in thee." There emerges within the heart a "holy desire," a longing for the text, the word of God to be concretized in reality.

4. Enter into Contemplation (*Contemplatio*)

Contemplatio shifts praying the Scripture into "a new language (silence)." This silence does not ask us to do anything, it is a call to *being*.

Robert E. Webber, *Journey to Jesus, The Worship, Evangelism, and Nurture Mission of the Church* (Nashville: Abingdon Press, 2001), 113.

APPENDIX 5

Worship Leader vs. Lead Worshiper

THERE IS A DISCUSSION within Evangelical circles today concerning the ordering of the words "Worship Leader" as opposed to "Lead Worshiper." You may be asking, "Is there really a difference, and if so, what is it?" The answer is, yes, there is a difference, and it is a big one.

The lead worshiper models worship, showing people an example of how a worshiper should behave. While modeling is one aspect of worship leadership, it is not a complete picture of leadership. The lead worshiper is one of the congregation who just happens to be worshiping in front of others hoping they will join in. Although this is an admirable thought, it is not leadership, and could lead to unengaged worship experiences for many congregations.

The worship leader, on the other hand, actively leads the congregation in worship. Though the goal is for the worship leader to be able to join in worship with the congregation, like a nature guide enjoying the view along with those on the tour, the primary job of the worship leader is to actually lead the congregation on their quest of worshiping the Lord with heart, soul, mind and strength.

As those called to lead others in the actions of worship, worship leaders are held to a higher standard and therefore, must consider the leadership role as highly important and eternally significant. Worship leaders cannot simply stand in front of people hoping they will join in somewhere along the way. That is poor leadership and poor stewardship of what God has entrusted to the leader. The calling of the worship leader is to guide, usher, and encourage the congregation toward a response to God's many revelations of himself. God has revealed himself and the job of the Worship Leader is to help the congregation respond through acts of worship (music, prayer, meditation on Scripture, baptism, communion, etc.).

Throughout the Bible we see that leading corporately requires the action of actually leading. Leading by example can be a powerful action, but when leading corporately, verbal instruction is important to engage the congregation in meaningful worship experiences. Moses did not simply model worship. He instructed the people of Israel on how to respond to all of that which God was doing for them. David did not simply worship and hope that others would follow his lead. He appointed worship leaders to lead the people. Jesus himself did not simply model worship, but taught his disciples how to pray, how to observe communion . . . how to worship.

If God has called you to be a worship leader, do it. Don't just model worship; lead his people in worship. And maybe, just maybe, we'll all join together, in the presence of God, and stand in awe.

APPENDIX 6

Roadmaps For Worship
by Dr. Jim Altizer

A.C.T.S.
Praise to the Lord, the Almighty
Words by Joachim Neander

Psalm 113 commands all *servants* of the Lord to *praise the name of the Lord both now and forever more—from the rising of the sun to the place where it sets*: In other words, always and everywhere, not just on Sundays. This morning we will use the acronym "A.C.T.S." as the roadmap for our worship. My prayer is that this will become a roadmap for your daily worship throughout the week. A.C.T.S. stands for "Adoration, Confession, Thanksgiving, and Supplication."

ADORATION

Speak out loud some words of adoration, like "O God, You are great. God, You are mighty. You are _____."

O Come Let Us Adore Him
Words and Music by John F. Wade

CONFESSION

Take some silent moments to confess your personal sins.

Let's read Psalm 51 out loud:

Have mercy on me, O God, according to your unfailing love; according to your great compassion blot out my transgressions.
Wash away all my iniquity and cleanse me from my sin.
For I know my transgressions, and my sin is always before me.
Against you, you only, have I sinned and done what is evil in your sight; so you are right in your verdict and justified when you judge.
Surely I was sinful at birth, sinful from the time my mother conceived me.
Yet you desired faithfulness even in the womb; you taught me wisdom in that secret place.
Cleanse me with hyssop, and I will be clean; wash me, and I will be whiter than snow.
Let me hear joy and gladness; let the bones you have crushed rejoice.
Hide your face from my sins and blot out all my iniquity.
Create in me a pure heart, O God, and renew a steadfast spirit within me.
Do not cast me from your presence or take your Holy Spirit from me.
Restore to me the joy of your salvation and grant me a willing spirit, to sustain me.
Then I will teach transgressors your ways, so that sinners will turn back to you.
Deliver me from the guilt of bloodshed, O God, you who are God my Savior, and my tongue will sing of your righteousness.
Open my lips, Lord, and my mouth will declare your praise.
You do not delight in sacrifice, or I would bring it; you do not take pleasure in burnt offerings.
My sacrifice, O God, is a broken spirit; a broken and contrite heart, you, God, will not despise.
May it please you to prosper Zion, to build up the walls of Jerusalem.
Then you will delight in the sacrifices of the righteous, in burnt offerings offered whole; then bulls will be offered on your altar.

THANKSGIVING

1 Thessalonians 5:18 tells us to:
Give thanks in all circumstances, for this is the will of God in Christ for you.

We might be thankful *because* of our circumstances, or we might have to be thankful in *spite of* our circumstances. The command is to be thankful, so, picture each circumstance of your life; financial, relationship, vocation, health, etc., and cause yourself to give thanks to God.

My Heart Is Filled With Thankfulness
Words and Music by Keith Getty and Stuart Townend
©2003 Thankyou Music

SUPPLICATION

To supplicate is to beseech, to humbly or earnestly ask for. Are there things in your life that you need God to do? Ask Him. Are there people in your life that need His touch? Ask Him. Are there situations that are beyond your control? Ask, that it may be given. Seek, that you may find. Knock, that the door would be open.

Blessed Be Your Name
Words and Music by Matt Redman and Beth Redman
©2002 Thankyou Music

APPENDIX 7

Worship Script

by Walt Harrah

BUT WE SEE JESUS

Many of you have been impacted by our sermon series through the book of Hebrews. How do I know that? Isaiah tells us that God's word never fails to accomplish the purpose for which it was sent. It is always effective. As a church, we have been impacted, and you as an individual have been impacted. Following our time of worship, there will be an opportunity for a few of you to reflect. Be thinking and praying if the Lord wants you to say something.

> In the past God spoke to our forefathers through the prophets at many times and in various ways, but in these last days he has spoken to us by his Son, whom he appointed heir of all things, and through whom he made the universe.
>
> The Son is the radiance of God's glory and the exact representation of his being, sustaining all things by his powerful word. After he had provided purification for sins, he sat down at the right hand of the Majesty in heaven. So he became as much superior to the angels as the name he has inherited is superior to theirs.

HEBREWS 1:1-4

All Hail The Pow'r Of Jesus' Name
Words and Music by Edward Perronet

PRAYER

There is no limit to your power, Lord Jesus. You created this world that we so thoroughly enjoy, you surrounded us with endless beauty and complexity and textures and colors and endless variety, all the while sustaining created matter, so that all matter functions according to the laws you set in place.

By your great power you left heaven and came to earth as one of us, becoming fully human. You had the power to rise from the dead, to ascend back to heaven, to reassume the glory you temporarily set aside.

And now, seated at the right hand of the Father in heaven, you are our advocate, cheering us on, praying for us, speaking to the Father on our behalf, even as you keep the display of God's wrath on hold until this age has been given its fully allotted time. Angels sing your praises continuously, and we this morning gratefully add our praise and prayers to theirs. In the name of our Brother Jesus we pray. Amen.

CONGREGATIONAL GREETING

Psalm 8 reflects on God's greatness . . . .

When I consider your heavens, the work of your fingers, the moon and the stars, which you have set in place, what is man that you are mindful of him, the son of man that you care for him?

You made him a little lower than the heavenly beings and crowned him with glory and honor.

You made him ruler over the works of your hands; you put everything under his feet: all flocks and herds, and the beasts of the field, the birds of the air, and the fish of the sea, all that swim the paths of the seas.

O LORD, our Lord, how majestic is your name in all the earth!

PSALM 8:3-9

Indescribable

Words and Music by Laura Story

©2004 Laura Stories, sixsteps Music, worshiptogether.com songs

Here's how Eugene Peterson in Message puts the Hebrews 2 passage . . . .

> What is man and woman that you bother with them;
> why take a second look their way?
> You made them not quite as high as angels,
> bright with Eden's dawn light;
> Then you put them in charge
> of your entire handcrafted world.

We know all too well that mankind has done a lousy job being in charge. Heaven was not willing to stand idly by and do nothing about our misery. Jesus rolled up his shirtsleeves and decided to do something about our condition.

[ON SCREEN]

But we see Jesus, who was made a little lower than the angels, now crowned with glory and honor because he suffered death, so that by the grace of God he might taste death for everyone.

Very, Very Good

Words and Music by Walt Harrah

©2012 Seedsower Music, ASCAP

In bringing many sons to glory, it was fitting that God, for whom and through whom everything exists, should make the author of their salvation perfect through suffering. Both the one who makes men holy and those who are made holy are of the same family. So Jesus is not ashamed to call them brothers. He says, "I will declare your name to my brothers; in the presence of the congregation I will sing your praises." And again, "I will put my trust in him." And again he says, "Here am I, and the children God has given me."

Since the children have flesh and blood, he too shared in their humanity so that by his death he might destroy him who holds the power of death—that is, the devil—and free those who all their lives were held in slavery by their fear of death. For surely it is not angels he helps, but Abraham's descendants. For this reason he had to be made like his brothers in every way, in order that he might become a merciful and faithful high priest in service to God, and that he might make atonement for the sins of the people. Because he himself suffered when he was tempted, he is able to help those who are being tempted.

Great God Of Love
Words and Music by Charles Wesley; Arr. by Walt Harrah
©2008 Seedsower Music, ASCAP

OFFERING
(no song, begin Hebrews reflection)

Reflection
Allow the congregation to reflect on what God has been teaching them throughout the Hebrews series
(leaders take wireless handheld to those who want to share)

SERMON

The Church's One Foundation
Words and Music by Samuel Stone

Benediction

Directions for Singing

by John Wesley

from his preface to Sacred Melody, 1761

"That this part of Divine Worship may be more acceptable to God, as well as the more profitable to yourself and others, be careful to observe the following directions:

1. Learn these tunes before you learn any others, afterwards learn as many as you please.

2. Sing them exactly as they are printed here, without altering or mending them at all; and if you have learned to sing them otherwise, unlearn it as soon as you can.

3. Sing All—see that you join the congregation as frequently as you can. Let not a slight degree of weakness or weariness hinder you. If it is a cross to you, take it up and you will find a blessing.

4. Sing Lustily—and with good courage. Beware of singing as if you were half-dead or half-asleep; but lift up your voice with strength. Be no more afraid of your voice now, nor more ashamed of its being heard, than when you sang the songs of Satan.

5. Sing Modestly—do not bawl so as to be heard above or distinct from the rest of the congregation that you may not destroy the harmony,

but strive to unite your voices together so as to make one melodious sound.

6. Sing in time—whatever time is sung, be sure to keep with it. Do not run before and do not stay behind it; but attend closely to the leading voices and move therewith as exactly as you can and take care not to sing too slow. This drawling way naturally steals on all who are lazy; and it is high time to drive it out from among us and sing all our tunes just as quick as we did at first.

7. Above all sing spiritually—have an eye to God in every word you sing. Aim at pleasing Him more than yourself, or any other creature. In order to attend strictly to the sense of what you sing, and see that your heart is not carried away with the sound, but offered to God continually; so shall your singing be such as the Lord will approve here, and reward when he cometh in the clouds of heaven."

APPENDIX 9

Guidelines for Encouraging Congregational Song
by Brian Wren

1. Choose songs to engage the mind as well as the emotions.

2. Avoid sentimentality, whether classical or popular.

3. Choose transitional music suitable for the transition it is making.

4. Don't use songs to fill in time or pass the time.

5. Recognize the persuasive power of music and use it reverently; don't use evocative music to sway people's decisions.

6. Know the functional genres of congregational song, including:

   Hymn: A sequence of stanzas, able to develop a theme and reach a conclusion.

   Chorus: A short song that states a theme without developing it—for easy singing, repetition, and "uplift."

   Round: A type of chorus, giving the effects of part-song.

   Refrain: An end-of-stanza chorus summarizing the message of a congregational song or giving a moment of participation in a song sung to the congregation.

   Chant: Music permitting a text not written in verse to be sung by a congregation.

   Ritual song: A short, congregational utterance that moves the action of worship.

Spirit singing: Improvised congregational singing, usually based on a major chord.

7. Distinguish between "our songs" and "other people's songs," and allow the latter to speak about the faith, hope, and struggle of other Christians.

8. Be sure the worship space has acoustics helping congregational singers hear one another: pews, chairs, and floor are crucially important.

9. Have people sit so that they can see as well as hear others: circle, square, or rectangle are the best configurations.

10. Be sure that people sit close enough together to hear one another sing.

11. Discover, respect, and repeat the familiar.

12. Strategize how to teach and repeat new songs.

13. Find out and use people's favorite hymns and songs.

14. Think generationally, but not stereotypically.

15. Respect the contract of enjoyment.

16. Look over the lectionary wall.

17. When introducing a song, read the words aloud, and speak them to the congregation.

18. Unless a tune is instantly accessible, have the congregation hear it several times before singing it.

19. Teach new songs in happy social situations.

20. Sing short congregational songs on every possible occasion.

21. Connect the song repertoires of Sunday school, vacation Bible school, church camp, and worshiping congregation.

22. Don't teach anything that must be denied in order to grow.

23. Keep records of what is sung.

24. Choose congregational songs that are experientially, as well as liturgically, coherent.

25. Find or become a song leader: a visible human being is the best teacher.

26. Believe in your own voice as a teaching instrument.

27. Believe that others can enjoy singing as much as you do, and show that you believe in them.

28. Teach new songs before the service begins, not during worship.

29. Introduce a new song with enthusiasm; never with an apology.

30. Before teaching a new song, learn the melody by ear, and by heart.

31. Teach a new melody in recognizable sections.

32. Teach by having people hear you sing the melody, not see you look at the music.

33. Use your natural voice, and show that you love the song and want to share it.

34. Teach new songs without accompaniment.

35. Choose tunes within a range both low and high voices can sing.

36. Begin worship with songs of medium pitch.

37. Encourage strong, unison singing as the norm.

38. Have at least one unaccompanied congregational song per Sunday.

39. Remember the two most important questions for music leader: "Can you be heard?" and "Can you hear the congregation?"

40. Use the lowest possible level of amplification.

41. Use live musicians, not backing tapes.

Brian Wren, *Praying Twice: The Music and Words of Congregational Song* (Louisville: Westminster John Knox Press, 2000), 123–125.

Made in the USA
San Bernardino, CA
29 August 2017